Global Flashpoints 2016

Center for Strategic & International Studies
1616 Rhode Island Avenue, NW
Washington, Dc 20036
202-887-0200 | www.csis.org

Published by Rowman & Littlefield
A wholly owned subsidiary of The Rowman & Littlefield Publishing Group, Inc.
4501 Forbes Boulevard, Suite 200, Lanham, MD 20706

Unit A, Whitacre Mews, 26-34 Stannary Street, London SE11 4AB

ISBN 978-1-4422-5188-5 (cloth alk. paper)
ISBN 978-1-4422-5189-2 (paperback)
ISBN 978-1-4422-5190-8 (electronic)

The paper used in this publication meets the minimum requirements of American National Standard for Information Sciences—Permanence of Paper for
Printed Library Materials, ANSI/NISO Z39.48-1992.

Printed in the United States of America

Global Flashpoints 2016

Editors
Craig Cohen
Melissa Dalton

CSIS | CENTER FOR STRATEGIC &
INTERNATIONAL STUDIES

ROWMAN & LITTLEFIELD
Lanham • Boulder • New York • London

Contents

INTRODUCTION
Craig Cohen

Washington think tanks exist and operate in a marketplace of ideas. A few of these ideas eventually become policy. Most do not. Like any entrepreneurial venture, there is no magic formula for success.

Because of the muddiness of the policymaking process, a sense of mystery surrounds think tanks. Many people do not understand what a think tank does, how it operates, or what role it plays in a policy setting. This leads some to exaggerate their influence, and others to ascribe negative motives or methods.

This confusion derives in part from a focus that is almost uniformly on the supply side of the equation—how think tanks seek to have influence. To understand why think tanks are the way they are, one must begin with the demand side. Why do think tanks exist in the first place?

If you are a government official, foreign policy reporter, corporate representative with an international ambit, or civil society representative, a major part of your job is understanding what is happening in the world, what is happening in Washington, and what is likely to change in the coming months and years ahead. Despite the gigabytes of information at everyone's fingertips, answering these questions is becoming harder, not easier.

There is not a Washington consensus on many policy prescriptions today, but there is broad agreement on the complex nature of the environment that exists and how it resists simple solutions.

Almost every think tank report will tell you that today's world is not binary, static, or predictable. Problems are multidimensional, and there is a high degree of complexity. The pace at which people and ideas circulate is rapidly accelerating. Secrecy is more difficult to ensure—not just for government but for the private sector as well. Trust in institutions is at an all-time low.

For your average official in Washington, there is too much noise, too many issues to cover, and too little time to think strategically. It is difficult to know where to turn for ground truth given the polarization of our domestic politics. The private sector, which may have been a source of credible outside advice in the past, is increasingly distant from government. And today's budget realities do not lend themselves to integrated, innovative thinking, instead breeding caution and infighting.

People look out their windows and see uncertainty and risk rather than opportunity. In essence, this is why people are turning more and more to think tanks like CSIS. They want help making sense of the world. They want help understanding the politics of Washington. They want a neutral, trusted space where they can meet with people outside of their own circles to exchange ideas in civil discourse. They want help formulating strategy. They want to do what 50 years ago could have been done within government itself or within informal networks, but today, too often, cannot.

Think tanks exist because the current world demands it.

The currency of think tanks is ideas, so what ideas can you find within this slim volume? Global Forecast is meant to provide a window into CSIS's collective thinking as we enter 2016, providing insight into the major ideas, events, trends, and personalities likely to shape international affairs in the year ahead.

Let me suggest three broad themes that I think you will find running through this anthology.

The first is the importance of history. Today, you are more likely to find international affairs scholars skilled at regression analysis than those with a deep historical understanding of a particular region. But what emerges from these articles is a sense of how important it is to know something about the ancient tributary system of China, early Islamic history, or competing anti-totalitarian and anti-colonial narratives of the 20th century if one wants to understand our modern challenges.

The second theme that emerges is the vital role economics plays in shaping today's security environment. Has there been a recent phenomenon with greater geopolitical implications than the emergence of China's middle class from rural poverty? This has fundamentally transformed the global economy and created conditions that have led to China's growing role on the world stage. Economics also stands at the center of U.S. strategy toward Asia, U.S. sanctions policy toward Russia and Iran, and the way low oil prices and the global decarbonization movement are altering geopolitical relationships. And economics is essential to understanding how much 'defense' the United States and its allies can afford to buy and how much is enough to achieve our goals now and in the future. Gone are the days when security experts can overlook economic causes and consequences.

The third theme you will find is the importance of leadership. Time and again, we are reminded of issues that require an "affirmative political strategy" such as ending the violence in Syria, or countering Putin's propaganda in Europe, or addressing a humanitarian crisis like Ebola. We often focus on the structural conditions that make any complex problem difficult to solve, but what runs strongly through this volume is the notion that leaders matter. Human agency matters. Ideas matter.

It is not predetermined whether the next decade will see the United States in retreat or fully engaged in the world. Our history may provide likely pathways, and our relative economic strength may determine what will be possible, but our leaders, with public support, will decide ultimately what the 21st century will bring.

Think tank experts are not fortune-tellers or weathermen. They are not in the prediction business. But they do seek to anticipate and explain occurrences based on an expert's eye for discerning the signal through the noise. There is a lot of noise in an election year. We hope the short essays in this volume will help you to keep focused on what will matter most to America's and the world's security and prosperity in the years ahead.

PART I
Geostrategy

1. Reconnecting of Asia

John J. Hamre

Four hundred years ago, the first genuinely international system of states in human history emerged. Prior to that time, there were regional geopolitical systems such as the various Chinese dynasties interacting with neighboring kingdoms. But there were no genuinely international systems. The Westphalian system created something quite new when nation states emerged. Personal loyalties were transferred from fealty to a king to a national identity and commitment to a state. The era also witnessed new organizational concepts, such as limited-liability corporations that broadly mobilized capital to focus it on targeted mercantilist ventures.

These European nation states sought to compete by creating globe-spanning empires to generate riches to support metropolitan centers. An international geopolitical system was born, centered in Europe, based on balance of power as an operating modality and grounded on mercantilist principles.

But there was a collateral consequence of this development. European empires sought commercial outposts around the world. The economic dynamism of this system pulled entrepreneurial impulses in Asia and Africa to the coastline. Naval transportation became the foundation of global commerce, giving rise to the great cities of Asia located on coastlines and along key waterways. And for the past 400 years, the geopolitical focus in Asia centered on the littoral.

Prior to this time, commerce and geopolitics in Asia were internal to the Eurasian continent. Interstate commerce coursed along the so-called "silk routes."

Today, this 400-year epoch of Asian geopolitics focused on the littoral is changing. The great Eurasian supercontinent is reconnecting internally. Russia has announced ambitious plans to create a modern rail network connecting the Far East with Europe. China has announced even more ambitious plans under the "One Belt, One Road" set of initiatives that would dramatically expand transportation networks through Central Asia into Western Asia. China has added a set of impressive and ambitious initiatives such as the Asian Infrastructure Investment Bank and the Silk Route Fund. Dozens of major infrastructure projects have been announced, giving operational direction to this sweeping initiative.

The One Belt, One Road (OBOR) initiative has stimulated wide-ranging debate. Some analysts voice skepticism, casting OBOR as an effort to stimulate development in China's lagging interior. Others see it as the next phase of pump priming, instigated by the now huge Chinese construction industry that is seeing slacking urban construction opportunities at home. And others see it as a grand geopolitical gesture designed to capture the loyalties of Central Asian countries, cementing them into vassal structures.

What does OBOR mean for the United States? Will OBOR consume the energies of China for the next few decades and ease pressure in Southeast Asia, or does OBOR reflect an all-encompassing agenda of Chinese hegemony throughout the vast Asian continent? Is OBOR good for America or a threat to our interests?

The new silk route narrative has been in circulation for many years. Over half of the "new silk route" entries in a web search trace back to Turkey and reflect Turkish commercial interests. There is no doubt that OBOR has geopolitical dimensions, but failing to see the underlying commercial dynamics would distort our analysis. The most efficient way to connect Asian producers to European markets in recent memory has been via sea transport. But overland rail links could easily cut transportation times by a factor of two or three. Cutting transit times dramatically would lower working capital demands by significantly reducing time when invested capital is unproductive.

The U.S. government is ill equipped to assess this macro-development. From a bureaucratic standpoint, we divide the world in ways that block clearer vision. The State Department divides this space into four bureaus—East Asia and Pacific Affairs, European and Eurasian Affairs, Near Eastern Affairs, and South and Central Asian Affairs. The Defense Department divides itself into a Pacific Command that includes China in its area of responsibility, but the Central Command and the European Command are responsible for other portions of Greater Asia.

Bureaucratic institutions channel creative thinking. We are ill equipped to perceive a mega-trend when we look at it from four different perspectives, seeing the attributes of a new dynamic only through distant historic filters.

It would be a huge mistake to ignore the significance of the reconnecting of Eurasia. It would be equally dangerous to cast it as a geopolitical threat to the United States. We have a limited role in shaping this mega-development, but we certainly could alienate ourselves from the central actors involved in it. We have time to assess this objectively. It should be on any agenda for the next presidency.

PART II
U.S. Strategy

2. America's Changing Role in the World

Kathleen H. Hicks

Every day, it seems Americans awaken to a crisis signifying a world out of their control. In Europe, our allies and partners are coping with Russian aggression, ranging from cyber attacks and energy coercion to conventional military might and a renewed emphasis on nuclear weapons. At the same time, Europe grapples with the world's most significant migration crisis since World War II. In Asia, satellite images of China's aggressive island-building activities are widely viewed as corroborating that nation's designs to control the air and sea space far from its shores. Meanwhile, North Korea's Kim Jong-un continues his family's legacy of dangerous provocations and nuclear ambition. As significant as the security situation is in these two regions, no area of the world is in greater tumult than the Middle East. From the destabilizing role of Iran to the chaos of Libya to the complete destruction of Syria and its implications for Iraq, Jordan, Turkey, and beyond, the upheaval appears endless.

The international system is shifting in ways not yet fully understood. Critics have pointed out the Obama administration's failure to articulate its vision for the U.S. role in a world evolving along so many dimensions. Yet the administration is not alone: no significant historian, analyst, or politician has done so either, including the administration's harshest critics. Policymakers should keep three factors in mind when devising such a vision.

The first key factor shaping the role of the United States today is the paradox of enduring superpower status combined with lessening global influence. The United States will likely remain the world's sole superpower for at least the next 15 years. The nation boasts enviable demographics, economics and innovation, natural resources, cultural reach, and of course military power. At the same time, its ability to shape the behavior of other actors is lessening.

How well the United States can wield power, and how much it chooses to do so, will vary by region and issue. Nonstate problems, for instance, are particularly difficult to tackle with existing U.S. foreign policy tools. Moreover, driving long-term solutions, such as improved governance capacity in places like Iraq, takes a generational investment and typically a whole-of-government and multinational approach. The United States has proven neither particularly patient for nor adept at such lengthy and multilateral strategies. On the other hand, where there is an assertive nation-state competitor—such as Iran, Russia, North Korea, and China—traditional U.S. security strengths tend to be more influential. Even in these cases, however, the United States has had difficulty deterring a wide range of provocations and coercive actions that run counter to its security interests.

A second factor that should inform the vision for U.S. foreign policy is the constancy of American public support for international engagement. If there is a theme in American grand strategy that has persisted for the past 70 years, it is that taking a leading role in the world is generally to the benefit of U.S. interests. Those interests have themselves remained remarkably consistent: ensuring the security of U.S. territory and citizens; upholding treaty commitments, to include the security of allies; ensuring a liberal economic order in which American enterprise can compete fairly; and upholding the rule of law in international affairs, including respect for human rights. Each presidential administration has framed these interests somewhat differently, and of course each has pursued its own particular path in seeking to secure them, but the core tenets have not varied significantly. An isolationist sentiment will always exist in American politics, but it is unlikely to upend the basic consensus view that what happens elsewhere in the world can affect us at home.

Equally important is a third factor that policymakers should take into account: a selective engagement approach to U.S. foreign policy is unavoidable. Despite the enduring, modern American consensus for international engagement, the United States has never had the wherewithal nor the desire to act everywhere in the world, all the time, or with the same tools of power. We have always had to weigh risks and opportunity costs and prioritize. The current budget environment makes this problem harder, and realizing greater security and military investment, through increased budgets and/or more aggressive institutional reforms and infrastructure cost cuts, should be pursued. Nevertheless, when it comes to the use of American force to achieve our ends, we should be prepared to surprise ourselves. As Robert Gates famously quipped in 2011, we have a perfect record in predicting our next crisis—we've never once got it right. Democracies, including the United States, can prove remarkably unpredictable. Policymakers need to understand this reality and not lead the public to expect a universal template that governs when and where the nation may act in support of its interests.

The paradox of superpower status and lessening influence, the American inclination toward international engagement, and the near-inevitability of selective engagement are realities that American policymakers and would-be presidents would be wise to understand. Discerning the shifting nature of the international system, and designing an effective set of American security tools within it, are monumental tasks, but they are not unprecedented. It is the same task that faced "the wise men" who helped shape the U.S. approach to world affairs at the end of World War II. Our circumstances today are equally daunting, requiring a similar reexamination of our strategies and capabilities for securing U.S. interests. Ensuring the nation is prepared to lead effectively—and selectively—will require leadership from Washington and partnership with likeminded nations and entities around the world.

3. Seeking the Right Strategy for Our Time

Michael J. Green

THe United States appears to be on the defensive everywhere. China has embarked on an aggressive reclamation and fortification program in the South China Sea and is calling for a new Eurasian order that would diminish U.S. alliances. Russia continues to defy NATO by deploying regular forces inside Ukraine and now Syria. Iran, despite a tenuous agreement on nuclear issues, arms proxies across the Middle East in pursuit of undiminished, irredentist objectives. The Islamic State's pursuit of a violent and repressive caliphate has been blunted, but hardly reversed. Meanwhile, international cooperation on climate change has faltered in advance of the Conference of the Parties (COP) 21 meeting in Paris in December and will fall well short of the initial goals of the Obama administration.

If ever there was a need for a coherent American grand strategy, it is now. But is the United States capable of formulating and implementing grand strategy? Grand strategy requires a clear definition of threats and objectives; the prioritization of efforts; and the integration of diplomatic, informational, military, and economic means in pursuit of those objectives. The American democratic system is designed to contest such centralization of decisionmaking and authority in one branch of government. As de Tocqueville observed:

A democracy can only with great difficulty regulate the details of an important undertaking, persevere in a fixed design, and work out its execution in spite of serious obstacles. It cannot combine its measures with secrecy or await their consequences with patience.[1]

And yet, the United States has repeatedly formulated and implemented successful grand strategies throughout the Republic's history in spite of the Founders' suspicion of European institutions and intrigue. The American government settled favorable borders in the Western Hemisphere by the late-middle 19th century; became a major power in the Pacific at the turn of the century; consolidated democratic alliances in Europe and Asia after the Second World War; and peacefully defeated Soviet communism 25 years ago. Only rarely were these strategies pursued through the agency of one man—a Theodore Roosevelt or Henry Kissinger. Instead, American grand strategy flowed from a "metaprocess that links ends and means effectively but not efficiently."[2] As John Ikenberry observes, successful strategies have been sustained abroad in the postwar era precisely because of the openness and contestation of political institutions at home, which empower and often reassure stakeholders in an American-led international order.[3] What de Tocqueville saw as a fatal flaw was in fact a great strength.

There are times, however, when the American democratic process becomes too contested and alarms rather than reassures allies and partners. There are also times when American political leaders succumb to doubt about the nation's ability to lead in world affairs. In the traumatic aftermath of the First World War and Vietnam, the American public chose leaders who eschewed geopolitics as the basis for American engagement in the world. In

---

[1] Alexis de Tocqueville, *Democracy in America* (New York: Vintage, 1945), 240-245 cited in Walter A. McDougall, "Can the United States Do Grand Strategy," remarks before the Foreign Policy Research Institute, April 2010.

[2] Richard K. Betts, "Is Strategy an Illusion?," *International Security* 25, no. 2 (Autumn 2000): 43.

[3] See John Ikenberry, *After Victory: Institutions, Strategic Restraint, and the Rebuilding of Order after Major Wars* (Princeton, NJ: Princeton University Press, 2001); and John Ikenberry, *Liberal Leviathan: The Origins, Crisis, and Transformation of the American System* (Princeton, NJ: Princeton University Press, 2011).

the wake of the Iraq War, the national mood again swung in that direction. The guiding themes for foreign policy strategy became "restoring America's global reputation"; focusing on transnational threats rather than geopolitics; a binary choice between "war" and "engagement"; a reactive incrementalism based on the principle, "don't do stupid stuff."

All of these post–Iraq instincts downplayed the importance of the nation state, of power balances, and of contestation over emerging regional orders in Asia, Eastern Europe, and the Middle East. China, Russia, and Iran have filled these "grey zones" between war and engagement with coercive strategies designed to diminish American influence and marginalize U.S. allies. (A similar argument could be made with respect to Latin America, though the revisionist states' threat to international order in that region is less significant.) Engagement of Moscow, Beijing, and Tehran on areas of mutual interest has had merit, but by presenting this engagement as a "grand strategy" in itself, the Obama administration has reinforced the impression that it is ceding the initiative on regional order to the revisionist powers. On the other hand, realists who argue for purely competitive strategies vis-à-vis these states ignore the complex position of allies and partners who, in most cases (particularly with Russia and China), are not prepared to sign on to a zero-sum strategy evocative of the Cold War. U.S. grand strategy must therefore restore geopolitics as the foundational understanding of state-to-state relations, but recognize that leadership depends on projecting credible diplomatic, economic, military, and values-based alternatives rather than trying to block regional states' relations with rising or revisionist powers in their neighborhood.

It goes without saying that sustaining economic growth at home is indispensable to this leadership role abroad, but that should not be an excuse for retrenchment. The United States does not have the option of leaving a contested world order to go to the gym for a few years and then return to the fray. In fact, many of the near-term steps that would enhance American influence abroad will also add dynamism to the U.S. economy at home. The Trans-Pacific Partnership (TPP) and Trans-Atlantic Trade and Investment Partnership (TTIP) will increase U.S. exports and establish new rules that bond Europe and the Pacific more closely to the United States. A renewed emphasis on promoting good governance, women's empowerment, rule of law, and civil society will create more just, stable, and prosperous societies abroad, with active consumers and better protection of intellectual property rights. Ending sequestration and enhancing security partnerships will allow sane strategic planning for corporations and more productive development of new systems and technology with allies and partners. Most states in the system want more economic and defense cooperation with the United States, not less. In fact, there has probably never been a period in modern history where this was so much the case. The larger question is whether Washington can prioritize and integrate these instruments of economic, normative, and military engagement to take advantage of this new trend.

Much will depend on the instincts of the American people. History is instructive on this question. In Gallop polls in the early 1920s a large majority of the American public said it was a mistake to have joined in the Great War. Over the next decade the Congress blocked defense spending and passed protectionist tariffs. By the late 1930s—as Japan and Germany began threatening order in Europe and the Pacific—the Gallop poll numbers reversed and a large majority of Americans began replying that the nation had been right to fight two decades earlier. FDR passed the Reciprocal Trade Agreements Act and began recapitalizing the Navy. In the mid-1970s as the public turned against the Vietnam War, Congress slashed defense spending and hamstrung the president's conduct of foreign policy. Less than a decade later—after unprecedented Soviet expansionism in the Third World—the American public rallied behind policies that increased defense spending, reversed Soviet advances, and laid the foundation for the end of the Cold War.

Polls today suggest a similar rebounding of American internationalism may be underway. National security has returned a top-tier issue for Republicans, while Pew polls show that a large majority of Americans now support TPP. Much will depend on leadership. Despite the rambunctious populism of the early primary process in both parties, there is reason to believe that the candidates making the strongest case for international engagement will ultimately prevail.

4. The Challenge to U.S. Leadership

James A. Lewis

> It has been a long and hard fight, and we have lost. This experience, unique in the history of the United States, does not signal necessarily the demise of the United States as a world power. The severity of the defeat and the circumstances of it, however, would seem to call for a reassessment of the policies . . . which have characterized much of our participation.

This was the final message from Thomas Polgar, last station chief in Saigon, and while we are unlikely to see helicopters landing on the roofs of embassies in Kabul or Baghdad, his words again apply to the situation in which America may soon find itself. A postmortem of how we got here is useful only if it guides us in the anarchic world that America now faces.

Repairing the damage to American influence from Vietnam took almost a decade. This time it will be harder. In 1975, America faced a monolithic and sluggish competitor. Europe's leaders needed American support against the Soviet Union. China and the major countries of the global south were not yet powerful nor did they actively seek to play a role in international affairs. Now we face many challengers whose only common characteristic is a desire to expand their influence, often at the expense of the United States and its faltering allies.

America may be the only global superpower, but in most regions it is actually in second or third place. Brazil dominates South America. Russia seeks to restore its control over its "near abroad." China pursues regional "hegemony," and India has capabilities that are the envy of any European power. South Africa, Turkey, Iran, and others maneuver and compete for regional advantage and leadership. If we concentrate our full resources in any region, the United States is overpowering, but the global scope of our concerns limits our ability to do this—we face requirements, sometimes self-imposed, that our competitors do not. The experience of Iraq and Afghanistan shows that even overwhelming military power does not always bring happy results.

Unlike the Cold War, we are not in a global contest. We are in a series of regional contests, some military, some not. America doesn't have a strategy for this new environment. Nor do we have strategic thinking to create that strategy. If we did have strategic thinking, someone might have realized that the 13-year effort to bring democracy and gender equality to the Middle East would produce chaos. These are undoubtedly noble goals, but the result is two wars that the United States won quickly and then lost, and not from a lack of commitment or resources.

China's Asian Infrastructure Investment Bank (AIIB) illustrates the problem of America's lack of influence, even as it concerns idealistic goals. Slowing climate change is a U.S. priority. Development is the priority for India, Brazil, and others. The International Monetary Fund and World Bank, led by the United States, won't lend for coal-fired or nuclear power plants. The AIIB will. Countries like India need dozens of new power plants in the next decade if they are to grow—not wind farms or solar panels. A bungled response to the new bank and congressional obtuseness on the value of the Export-Import bank means we are taking ourselves, and the global institutions created in 1945, out of the running. The effect is to pass the baton to China.

"Responsibility to protect" can often sound like "Right to invade" to audiences in the global south. The seminal experience that shapes and justifies Western policy is the long struggle against totalitarianism. The seminal experience for non-Western countries is the long struggle against Western colonialism and it is through this prism that they interpret our various interventions.

Each region calls for a tailored strategy and a recognition of the strengths and limits of U.S. power. This strategy will require decisions on what we want—and some regions are more important than others—and what we can expect to get. Some regions will require confrontation, others cooperation, and a few can be left to their own devices. Coercion will rarely work and preaching is not really an option. The challenge lies with building a coherent global approach to regional efforts and resources to support them.

This is not a lament for the demise of American power. America lacks a strategy for this new environment, but size, population, and wealth guarantee that the United States will always be in the top tier of countries. Leadership is another matter. Two related leadership crises mean that America will punch below its weight. The political turmoil that paralyzes Congress is so severe as to qualify as a constitutional crisis. The political crisis is matched by intellectual weaknesses in what might be called the foreign policy "nomenklatura," a weakness compounded by ideological politics and irrelevant academic debate.

It is not clear that the nomenklatura realizes or admits that while our military has not been defeated, we have lost. The easy assumption of indispensable global power and responsibility that followed the Cold War should be shattered by events since 2002, but it remains a comfortable refuge from hard thinking about the difficult choices. We must temper an ideological agenda for social change with actions to build and sustain influence, and between old allies and new powers. This choice is neither new nor black and white, but it can no longer be made on the assumption of easy and automatic power. Its permanent members are the victors of 1945, not necessarily today's great powers.

U.S. global leadership is not immutable, and it has been severely injured since 2001. Leadership did not come from military power or busy interventions, but from powerful ideas and from creating international rules and institutions to implement them. Now these rules and institutions are being challenged—some want to replace them, others seeking only to gain what they see as their rightful place. The intellectual core of American policy—democracy, self-determination, rule of law—remains strong, but needs sustained engagement (not an occasional visit) with new powers if they are to remain persuasive to a world where power has shifted away from the North Atlantic. Overconfidence and unrealistic goals have damaged America in the world; with pragmatism and luck, we can recover.

PART III
Middle East

5. ISIS (Re)Writes History

Jon B. Alterman

Deterrence History, we are often told, is written by the winners. Modern states and peoples are the products of success; historians seek the origins of their glory. The victors make it easy: they leave voluminous records and they ransack the records of those they have defeated.

What would history written by losers look like? It would look a lot like the history that the Islamic State is writing now.

Islamic history has a good amount of winning in it. Not only did medieval Muslim armies conquer lands from Spain to India, but Muslim traders spread the religion still further into the Far East and Southeast Asia. For centuries, Islamic math and science led the world, and Muslim scholars helped preserve the manuscripts of antiquity. Renaissance scholars relied on them as they rediscovered ancient Greece and Rome.

This winning is not central to the historiography of the Islamic State. The group's followers swim in a sea of victimhood, resentment, and vengeance, and they luxuriate in paranoia and xenophobia. The group's central organizing truth is not about the power Muslims hold but instead the power that Muslims have lost. Grievance motivates them, and it is precisely the group's abject weakness that drives and legitimates its most barbaric acts against symbols of global power. If one looks at the Islamic State's videos, a single theme is overwhelming. The Islamic State desperately seeks equivalence to infinitely stronger and more capable foes. Its imagery is all about promoting feelings of agency among its fighters; often it is accompanied by an effort to enfeeble a symbol of some hostile force.

The Islamic State did not invent the instrumentalization of history. Saddam Hussein reveled in the symbolism of Babylonia, and the Shah of Iran sought to tie himself to Persepolis and the empire of Cyrus the Great. Benito Mussolini sought to rebuild the glories of Rome, and Ataturk moved Turkey's capital from cosmopolitan Constantinople to the Anatolian heartland in order to engender an "authentic" Turkish identity.

What the Islamic State is doing is different, though. It is more like Adolph Hitler's reliance on—and sometimes invention of—Aryan history to inspire and guide a modern society. Common to both projects is the passionate marriage between a utopian social vision and a conspiratorial worldview—a society locked in endless battle against myriad enemies. The utopian vision inspires, and enemies help preserve solidarity. History helps bind the two.

But it is a certain kind of history at play. Real history is chaotic, messy, and full of ambiguity. Its lessons are hard to discern, when they can be discerned at all. The history peddled by these groups is different. It is streamlined, possessing a clear moral objective and a clear enemy. It not only projects legitimacy on its adherents, but it connects them to an eternal truth. Groups use this kind of history to grasp at immortality. In her book, *The Future of Nostalgia*, the scholar Svetlana Boym discusses how history can permit the "transformation of fatality into continuity." Everyday acts can be sanctified because they are invested with the spirit of lost generations. Each generation struggles to remain as true to its ancestors as the preceding generation did, despite the temptations of innovation and modernity.

Some of these traditions have shallower roots than one might suppose. More than three decades ago, Eric Hobsbawm and Terence Ranger gathered a series of spectacular nineteenth-century efforts to weave modern traditions from the threads of historical evidence. Perhaps most colorful example was the Victorian effort to create a unified Scottish culture full of kilts and proprietary clan tartans. The truth was much more of a muddle, involving cloth merchants and a rising sense of Scottish nationalism.

Adherents to the Islamic State are engaged in a spectacular act of invention, seeking to dress their modern reign in ancient garments. They insist on the timelessness of what they claim to be ancient and holy customs, and they harshly punish those who depart from those customs. But are those customs really ancient and holy? One of the most visible symbols of Islamic practice, women's veiling, certainly is not commanded in the Quran, and it is largely an interpretation of the privacy afforded to women in the Prophet Muhammad's family.

Did the Prophet Muhammad lash his followers for smoking cigarettes? He couldn't have, as cigarettes were invented more than 1,200 years after his death, and tobacco itself did not come to the Middle East until 950 years afterwards. Bans on television, recorded music, soccer games, and the like all reflect innovations.

What the Islamic State is, in fact, is a wholly modern movement that seeks to be ancient. Like the photo booths in tourist towns that produce sepia-toned photographs of contemporary subjects in period clothing, its wink toward the present is part of its appeal. Its followers are not recreating a holy seventh-century society of pious believers. They are gathering the dispossessed and disaffected to an invented homeland that strives to provide certainty, intimacy, and empowerment to a population that feels too little of any of them.

There is little use quibbling with their distortions of history, which are too numerous to mention. Instead, what is risible is their solemn use of history at all. This group is wholly modern and wholly innovative. It is wholly disruptive, as it seeks to be. Its followers should not be ennobled by their purported connection to history.

Western governments and their allies in the Middle East should not fall into the trap of seeing the Islamic State and its like as groups hostile to modernity. Instead, they should highlight how truly modern these groups are, and how selective they are in their readings of history. They do not guide their followers back to the well-worn path of tradition, but instead blaze a new trail of confrontation with the rest of the world.

Stripped of their historical costumes, we can see them as they are: the angry and the weak, preying on those even weaker than themselves.

There is glory to be found in Islam. It is not to be found in them.

6. Wanted: A U.S. Strategy for Syria and Iraq

Melissa G. Dalton

Fifteen months since the U.S.-led coalition began its campaign against the Islamic State in Iraq and Syria (ISIS), ISIS remains a formidable force in both countries. Although coalition airstrikes and local forces have taken back some territory in the northern regions, ISIS maintains military momentum, continues to lure recruits internationally, and retains control of substantial areas in Syria's north and east and Iraq's west.

Meanwhile, Russia's airstrikes in Syria, backed by Iranian-supported local ground forces, buttress the foundering Assad regime by targeting Syrian opposition groups, broadly defined—including some that have received U.S. assistance. U.S. efforts to train and equip Syrian opposition forces have been painfully slow and set back by attacks from the Assad regime and militant groups.

In Iraq, deep Sunni doubt over Baghdad's commitment to an inclusive way forward have stalled coalition efforts to push ISIS out of key strongholds. The humanitarian consequences of these conflicts are profound, contributing to the world's largest wave of migration since World War II. The U.S.-led fight against ISIS is faltering because it has taken a narrow approach to a broader conflagration, addressing only the symptoms of a deep-rooted problem. The U.S. deployment of less than 50 special operations forces to northern Syria reflects a recognition that the campaign's ground component is faltering, but it will not fill the gap alone.

A major reason for ISIS's survival in its various incarnations since the mid-2000s is the lack of credible governance and security provided by Baghdad and Damascus for Sunni populations. ISIS's brutality attracts some recruits, but distances it from the vast majority of Muslims, and therein lies one of its vulnerabilities.

The Islamic State's mandate to secure territory and govern also presents a vulnerability, particularly given that, like many closed societies, it does not have a sustainable economic model. Reported food and fuel shortages and daily exhibitions of terror and violence evince the difficulties ISIS is facing in governing its territory. However, in the absence of an alternative political pathway for Sunnis in Iraq and Syria, ISIS will likely endure.

If the United States is to succeed in degrading support for ISIS, it must have an affirmative political strategy for Syria and Iraq. Degrading ISIS through military and economic tools is important, but this is only a supporting component of a strategy.

A political strategy does not have to involve a nation-building exercise, and the United States should certainly be wary of hubristic visions. The lessons of Iraq and Afghanistan should underscore prudence, and yet, reticence could be equally as damaging to U.S. interests. Rather, the United States should have a more balanced approach.

The United States and its partners must first work with Syrians and Iraqis to establish political and military structures at both the central government and local levels upon which these countries can build a viable framework of governance. There may be some hope of sewing together a decentralized but inclusive Iraq over the next several years, but mending Syria will take much longer.

Second, building on the momentum of concluding a nuclear deal with Iran, the P5+1, including Russia, should lead efforts to bring a political end to Syria's civil war. Any viable approach will likely require a multiyear transition, resulting in Assad eventually stepping down. This diplomatic effort would also need to engage Syrians, Iran, Saudi Arabia, and Turkey. A starting point for a Syrian political transition process is the framework developed at the 2012 Geneva talks, engaging not only expatriate Syrians but also local leaders identified by the aforementioned assessment process.

These diplomatic efforts would need to be coupled with the deployment of a multinational peacekeeping force to protect civilians and enable the passage of humanitarian aid and reconstruction assistance, likely through a secured buffer zone on Turkey's southern border with Syria.

A third leg of the strategy would involve rallying Gulf partners, Turks, and other Europeans to help Syrians build a credible security force capable of protecting civilians and countering terrorism. Channeling these efforts through a single stream rather than through conflicting ones, and coordinating those forces with the multinational peacekeeping force, would be critical to make the Syrian security force an enduring part of a new Syria.

Neither the peacekeeping force and buffer zone nor the building of Syrian security forces will succeed in the absence of a strong political framework for a new Syria.

In Iraq, the United States and its partners should press Baghdad to create a political framework for an inclusive and decentralized system of governance that addresses the grievances of Iraq's Sunnis, the aspirations of the Kurds, and the concerns of the Shi'a.

Within this framework, in addition to strengthening the Iraqi security forces, the United States and its Gulf partners should step up their support for Sunni tribal forces, coordinating with Baghdad but also working directly with the tribes to fund and expedite their training. The United States should also send additional military advisers to Iraq to assist with the training. Initially, Sunni tribal forces should be trained to protect civilians and deter further ISIS incursions into Iraqi territory. Over time, they could push ISIS out of Iraq's cities, coordinating their moves with coalition airstrikes.

Meantime, Russia will want to maintain its military foothold on the Mediterranean, and Iran will want to maintain its strategic resupply routes to Hezbollah and its influence in Iraq, and so the United States will have to decide whether those are prices worth accepting for Russian and Iranian pressure on Assad to step down. Increasing U.S. and partners' covert efforts to degrade Iranian proxy capabilities in the Levant and the Gulf, and building ties with Iraqis and the new Syrian political leadership, could mitigate some of those risks.

None of this will be easy nor come without costs. Yet keeping the focus solely on degrading ISIS is not a strategy, will not result in a durable solution to the conflicts in Syria and Iraq, and will further imperil U.S. interests. The next administration will need to tackle these challenges head on and offer an affirmative vision and strategy for moving out of the morass.

7. Iran After the Agreement

Anthony H. Cordesman

The political debates over the Iran nuclear agreement have tended to focus on side issues: what might happen more than 10 years from now, how soon Iran could develop one crude nuclear device, worst-case 24-day challenges to inspection, and largely irrelevant issues like the inspection of Parchim—an Iranian facility that has already been destroyed. Washington now must face both the challenges in actually implementing the Iran nuclear agreement and a much wider range of challenges from Iran.

Arms Control as an Extension of War by Other Means

The first step is going to be actually implementing the most critical phases of the Iran nuclear agreement. Unless Iran rejects the agreement or the U.S. Congress finds some truly inventive way to block it, almost all of the critical physical actions Iran must take have to be completed by what is called Implementation Day. Cutting back on enriched material, cutting centrifuge efforts, ending the ability of the Arak reactor to produce plutonium, radically changing the inspection process, dealing with the International Atomic Energy Agency (IAEA) question about past military activities, and creating a new process to control procurement will all have to be completed at some point in 2016, probably between the spring and mid-summer, and in the middle of a U.S. presidential campaign.

Really serious arms control agreements tend to be an extension of war by other means, and the United States will have to press hard to ensure full compliance, ensure that other countries will be ready to reintroduce sanctions if Iran cheats, and persuade Israel and our Arab allies that the agreement is really working. The Obama administration must implement at the same time as it prepares for the next administration. It must deal with Russia and China as well as its allies in the P5+1, and lay what groundwork it can for a more bipartisan approach.

It must also do so at a time when there are few indications that Iran's national security structure is in any way committed to some better relationship. Iran faces a February 2016 election of its own for its legislative assembly and Council of Experts where its conservatives seem to be pressing hard to restrict the number of moderate candidates. It is the Supreme Leader, not the president, who can veto, and who controls the military, the security structure, the intelligence branches, the justice system, and key elements of the media. So far the Supreme Leader has shown no interest in improved relations, has seriously questioned the value of the agreement and its current terms, nor done anything to shift Iran's efforts in other aspects of security.

This may come, but at least in the near term and probably though at least 2017 and the establishment of a new administration in the United States, Washington will have to make the agreement work in spite of Iranian reservations and willingness to "game" the arms control process and reduction in sanctions and do so at a time many other countries will be rushing to compete in Iran regardless of how the U.S. Congress reacts.

The Other Four Challenges

First, the United States will also have to focus on the other challenges posed by Iran, and all are now growing. Iran has been steadily improving its missile forces, increasing their range-payload, developing solid fuel rocket motors and more lethal conventional warheads, and greatly increasing their accuracy and ability to hit high-value point targets. It is working on cruise missiles and armed drones as well, and highly accurate conventional warheads can turn such missiles into "weapons of mass effectiveness" by striking critical infrastructure and military targets.

This means the United States has even more reason to help Israel develop its tiered system of missile and rocket defenses—Arrow 3, David's Sling, and Iron Dome—and help its Gulf allies develop a more effective mix of air defenses and wide-area missile defenses like THAAD (Terminal High-Altitude Area Defense) and Standard.

Second, the U.S. government must work with the Gulf Cooperation Council states to create an effective counter to Iran's steadily improving mix of asymmetric warfare forces that it can use to threaten shipping and petroleum exports through the Gulf. These involve advances in Iran's sea, air, and missile forces, and in areas that range from antiship missiles and suicide low-radar-profile speedboats to smart mines. This means deploying a new mix of U.S. ships and air assets, major arms transfer to Arab allies, and new efforts at training and joint exercises.

It also means restoring Arab confidence that the United States will stay in the Gulf and Middle East, will not somehow turn to Iran at their expense, and will give them the arms transfers and training help they need. It means showing them that Washington can and will act decisively to support them, that it has a clear strategy for dealing with Syria, Iraq, and Yemen, and that it really is committed to partnership in every aspect of both military security and counterterrorism—not simply selling arms and serving its own interests.

Third, the United States cannot let the tensions over the Iran nuclear agreement and political tensions between President Obama and Prime Minister Netanyahu create a situation that affects Israel's security. In 2007, the Bush administration and the Israeli government agreed to a memorandum of understanding that the United States would ensure an Israeli "edge" over the forces of any threat power, and a 10-year, $30 billion military aid package for the period from FY2009 to FY2018. President Obama stated in 2013 that the United States would continue such aid, but the present series of security agreements still needs to be formally renewed, and Washington must not only focus on the direct threat from Iran, but Iran's arms transfers and other aid to Hezbollah and Hamas.

Fourth, the United States must counter Iran's growing influence in four key countries: Lebanon, Syria, Iraq, and Yemen, as well as the increasing challenge it has posed in terms of contacts with the Shi'ites in the Arab Gulf states. The United States and Iran do have a limited common interest in fighting ISIS and other violent Sunni Islamist movements. It is important to remember, however, that Iran's revolution is a form of religious extremism, and it is seeking to boost Hezbollah in Lebanon, keep the Assad regime in power in Syria, increase its influence in Iraq and its ties to Shi'ite militias and the Iraqi security forces, and has attempted to send a nine-ship convoy to aid the Houthis in Yemen.

Looking Beyond Confrontation

There is a fifth challenge of a very different kind. The United States must mix these four security efforts with an approach to relations with Iran and sanctions that make it clear that Iran does have future options. The United States needs to make sure Iran actually receives the benefits of the lifting of nuclear sanctions if it fully complies with the nuclear agreement. The United States needs to work with Iran's Arab neighbors so it is always clear that Iran can actually improve its security by improving its relations with both the United States and Arab states.

The United States needs to explore ways to increase cultural and other exchanges if this becomes possible, and to reach out to Iranian moderates and the Iranian people. It needs to develop a broader range of negotiations and incentives for Iran to take a more moderate course in all the other areas that now present security challenges to the United States and its allies.

There may well be no immediate prospects for broader improvements in U.S.-Iranian relations, and Washington must never make such improvements in relations at the expense of its allies. At the same time, the nuclear agreement has shown that Iran does have a more moderate president and many other senior officials. A large portion of the Iranian people clearly do not see the United States as the "great Satan," and a number of Iranian officials and security experts do realize that Iran's real strategic interests lie in regional cooperation and dealing with the growing threat of religious extremism. The United States must never let the fact that the Supreme Leader and other Iranian hardliners demonize the United States lead the United States to demonize Iran. We must do everything we can to encourage Iran to change and evolve.

8. U.S.-Israel Ties After the Agreement

Haim Malka

People have dismissed tremors in the U.S.-Israeli partnership for more than a decade, yet beneath the surface the signs are clear. The tectonic plates of three core assumptions of the partnership are shifting. While an earthquake is not imminent, the topography of the relationship is changing in important ways.

First, America's defense commitment to Israel is becoming more difficult to ensure. Many supporters of Israel declare this as an iron-clad guarantee, and the United States has backed up its political declarations by spending almost $100 billion over a half-century to ensure that Israel's advanced weaponry gave it a qualitative military edge against its adversaries. The political commitment is so strong that the concept of Israel's qualitative military edge has been enshrined in U.S. law.

That aid has been crucial. U.S. support helped Israel neutralize conventional military threats from surrounding states and establish Israel as the dominant regional military force. Several of those states decided to make peace with Israel. Those countries that have been holding out have little illusion of ever defeating Israel on the battlefield, and even quietly cooperate.

The problem, however, is that Israel's primary threats are no longer conventional, but asymmetric threats from groups such as Hezbollah and Hamas, and potential ballistic missile strikes from Iran. Israeli military leaders predict that Hezbollah will fire thousands of missiles and rockets at Israeli cities in their next war. Such strikes would paralyze Israel's transportation and industrial infrastructure while putting millions of Israelis at risk.

Iran is a different kind of threat that many Israelis believe threatens their very existence. Israelis often worry that if Iran were to launch a nuclear weapon at Israel, they would at most have several minutes of warning. The idea of providing Israel with more advanced weapons platforms and ammunition such as the B-52 bomber and massive ordnance penetrators to mitigate Israeli anxiety and help smooth relations misjudges both the nature of Israel's threats and how Israelis perceive those threats. In reality, there is no weapon system or political guarantee that will cure Israel's anxiety on the Iranian nuclear threat.

Deterring surrounding Arab armies was relatively straightforward, but addressing these kinds of threats is increasingly difficult. In 2014, it took Israel seven weeks to subdue Hamas rockets, and doing so failed to change the strategic balance in Gaza. The problem is not all Israel's. U.S. military planners face their own challenges addressing asymmetric threats. In Iraq and Afghanistan, the United States deployed hundreds of thousands of troops and spent more than a trillion dollars to subdue nonconventional forces, but still struggled. While U.S. aid has helped Israel mitigate missile threats by building an integrated missile defense system, there is no commitment that can protect the Israeli home front or solve the deeper problems that asymmetrical and unconventional threats pose.

Second, the partnership faces a growing strategic disconnect. Israeli and American perceptions have never been in complete harmony, but there was enough of a common organizing principle to overcome different strategic perceptions and priorities. In the 1970s and 1980s they were bound by the Cold War, in the 1990s by the shared project of Arab-Israeli peace, and after the September 11, 2001, attacks the global war on terrorism brought them together.

Today's Middle East provides little of the same unity. Israel no longer fits into U.S. regional strategy as it once did, in part because there is no coherent strategy, but rather a series of policies. The problem for Israel is deeper, however. Israel fears that the United States is disengaging from the region and recalibrating its policy to cooperate more closely with Iran. That fuels Israeli anxiety over a regional leadership vacuum that will leave it more vulnerable at a time of rising Iranian influence.

The governments of the United States and Israel have fundamentally contradictory policies on Iran, in addition to multiple strategic disagreements on everything from Syria strategy to advanced U.S. weapon sales to Arab governments. Further, many of these challenges are only beginning. Verifying and implementing the Joint Comprehensive Plan of Action will cause ongoing tension and conflict over what constitutes Iranian violations and how to address them. And on top of all that, despite dim prospects for progress, the Palestinian issue will remain a fault line in U.S.-Israeli relations.

Third, Israel has once again become a partisan issue in American politics. It took Israel and its U.S.-based allies nearly four decades to turn U.S. support from a narrow partisan pursuit to a bipartisan staple of American politics. That consensus is breaking down, partly because the centers of Israeli domestic politics and U.S. domestic politics are diverging. The U.S.-Israel relationship was forged at a time when Israel was center-left, and Israel's subsequent rightward shift has not been matched consistently in the United States. Increasingly, the current Israeli government feels more comfortable with the Republican Party, and the prime minister rather publicly aligned with congressional Republicans in an effort to undermine the president's agenda on Iran. Congressional Democratic support for Israel remains strong, to be sure, but among the public, partisan differences on Israel are increasingly visible.

The next U.S. president will surely have warmer relations with Israel's prime minister, and upgraded levels of military assistance will help give the impression that the partnership has been reset. The U.S.-Israeli partnership will endure, but further tremors lie ahead. The two sides will not only need to manage those differences carefully, but also appreciate the ways in which the foundations on which the relationship was built are shifting.

PART IV
Russia, Europe, and Eurasia

9. Putin's Europe

Heather A. Conley

Imagine that a new parliamentary political faction is suddenly formed in the European Parliament consisting of 38 members from over eight European countries.[1] This faction's members have voted 93 percent of the time in favor of the Kremlin's positions and oppose the EU-Ukraine Association Agreement, support Russia's annexation of Crimea, and refuse to condemn the murder of Russian opposition leader Boris Nemtsov.

This isn't imagination; this is the Europe of Nations and Freedom (ENF) faction in the European Parliament, which was formed in June 2015 and is led by far-right French leader of Front Nationale, Marine Le Pen. Ms. Le Pen received a €9 million loan from the Moscow-based First Czech-Russian Bank last November.[2]

Now, imagine a Europe that has become increasingly dominated by Russian television, radio, and Internet sites. Local oligarchs, in collusion with the Kremlin, have purchased many of the continent's independent news outlets. Russian news outlets copy their Western media counterparts assiduously. They play popular music, provide human interest stories, report frequently on rampant corruption and decadence in the

1 Péter Krekó, Marie Macaulay, Csaba Molnár, and Lóránt Győri, "Europe's New Pro-Putin Coalition: The Parties of 'No,'" Institute of Modern Russia, August 3, 2015, http://imrussia.org/en/analysis/world/2368-europes-new-pro-putin-coalition-the-parties-of-no.

2 David Chazan, "Russia 'bought' Marine Le Pen's support over Crimea," *The Telegraph*, April 4, 2015, http://www.telegraph.co.uk/news/worldnews/europe/france/11515835/Russia-bought-Marine-Le-Pens-support-over-Crimea.html.

West, and play on the fears of extremism and nontraditional society, while sprinkling in "news" stories of fascists taking over in Ukraine and European leaders subservient to their U.S. masters.

This isn't fiction, either. This is the reality that has been created by increasingly sophisticated Russian news outlet, RT (formerly Russia Today). RT claims to reach over 700 million people[3] and has an annual budget comparable in size to the BBC's World News Service.[4] The United Kingdom's media regulator, Ofcom, has recently sanctioned RT for biased coverage of events in Ukraine.[5]

Finally, imagine a NATO country that is 95 percent dependent on Russian gas imports.[6] Russia directly owns three of this country's largest companies and a Russian investment arm recently purchased this country's largest telecommunications company. Further imagine that this country pays nearly twice as much for its gas than other European countries.[7] Despite this incredible dependency and high cost, this country has not built gas interconnectors to other European countries, constructed domestic energy storage facilities, or taken any meaningful steps to reduce its dependency on Russian energy. This country is Bulgaria today.

Welcome to Putin's Europe. How can the United States and Europe counter this reality?

The two most important actions that can be effectively deployed by the West against Russian influence in Europe would be both to recognize the depth of the problem and immediately enhance transparency of Western interactions with Russian companies and organizations. It is absolutely vital that the United States and Europe recognize the extent of the challenge.

[3] RT, "About RT," https://www.rt.com/about-us/.

[4] Josh Halliday, "BBC World Service fears losing information war as Russia Today ramps up pressure," *The Guardian*, December 21, 2014, http://www.theguardian.com/media/2014/dec/21/bbc-world-service-information-war-russia-today.

[5] Jasper Jackson, "RT sanctioned by Ofcom over series of misleading and biased articles," *The Guardian*, September 21, 2015, http://www.theguardian.com/media/2015/sep/21/rt-sanctioned-over-series-of-misleading-articles-by-media-watchdog.

[6] Georgi Kantchev, "Bulgaria Says Signs Natural Gas Link Deal with Romania, Greece," *Wall Street Journal*, April 22, 2015, http://www.wsj.com/articles/bulgaria-says-signs-natural-gas-link-deal-with-romania-greece-1429706460.

[7] Center for the Study of Democracy, "Energy Sector Governance and Energy (In)Security in Bulgaria," 2014, http://www.csd.bg/artShow.php?id=16984.

Although it was the policy of both the United States and Europe to help integrate Russia into Western structures, what Europe and the United States have failed to understand is that the Kremlin was using Western laws and institutions to extend its political and economic reach while simultaneously eroding European public support for democratically elected leaders and institutions. As much as President Putin has railed against a Western-organized "fifth column" in Russia, the Kremlin has been quite adept at creating one in Europe.

A classic example would be Russian investment patterns in Bulgaria. It might be surprising to know that the Netherlands, not Russia, is the largest foreign investor in Bulgaria (approximately 20 percent). No one would be particularly concerned about a concentration of Dutch investment, yet the Dutch are only the leading foreign investor because the Russian state-owned oil company, LukOil, has incorporated their holding company in the Netherlands. European countries must demand greater transparency of complex holding company structures that attempt to mask the Russian origin of investment. What LukOil has done is perfectly legal but it underscores the lack of recognition of the size and scale of the challenge.

There is also an urgent need for greater transparency and disclosure of the identities of government-sponsored backers of European political parties and how they are financed. It isn't simply the €9 million loan to Le Pen's Front Nationale that is of concern. The Kremlin is actively courting a variety of European xenophobic and far-right groups. Moscow has hosted Marine Le Pen as well as the leaders of Hungary's far-right, anti-Semitic Jobbik party and Bulgaria's far-right, nationalist party Ataka. This support is paying dividends. According to the Hungarian-based Political Capital Institute, far-right political parties in 15 EU states have publicly supported the Kremlin's policies and positions.[8] It is highly ironic that as Mr. Putin decries the rise of fascist tendencies in Europe, he is stoking and financially supporting them and thus encouraging their popularity. It also appears that as Mr. Putin has

---

[8] Political Capital Institute, "The Russian Connection: The Spread of pro-Russian Policies on the European Far Right," March 14, 2014, http://www.riskandforecast.com/useruploads/files/pc_flash_report_russian_connection.pdf.

perfected the art of "managed democracy" in Russia—where Russian authorities "arrange both the elections and the results"—the Kremlin is now attempting to "manage" several other European democracies.

It is also vital to recognize that all nongovernmental organizations (NGOs) in Europe, particularly those that are created seemingly overnight, are not created equal. Again and ironically, while Vladimir Putin has declared that Western-funded civil society organizations in Russia are "undesirables," Russian-created and -funded NGOs actively working in Europe are highly desirable as the Kremlin uses them to influence European public opinion and policy. The majority of Russian NGO funds—estimated to be approximately $100 million—support the implementation of Russia's compatriot-abroad policies and are funneled through the Russkiy Mir (Russian World) foundation and other individuals and organizations connected to the Kremlin.[9]

Yet perhaps the most difficult challenge is the West's ability to counter Russian propaganda. Despite our fond Cold War memories of the role played by Voice of America and Radio Free Europe in the former Warsaw Pact countries, the United States and Europe will never be able to "out-propagandize" Russia's sophisticated operations. Yet, there are ways to mitigate Russian media dominance. First, Europe should ensure that its media outlets are diversified and again, transparency will play a key role. For example, the Estonian Internet site baltiju.eu is operated by Altmedia, a firm that is funded by Media Capital Holding BV, registered in the Netherlands but owned by Russia state news agency, Rossiya Segodnya, according to the Estonian security service.[10] Second, the West must use those existing Russian social networks that remain open to channel factual news reports with the hope that this information will reach a certain portion of the Russian population.

Without substantial focus on this growing challenge, the transatlantic community's credibility and unity are at stake; for why would Russia need to cross a NATO border when the Kremlin can control a NATO country from the inside?

---

[9] "The Kremlin's Millions, and its support of pro-Russian activists in the Baltics," *The Baltic Times*, September 7, 2015, http://www.baltictimes.com/kremlin_s_millions/.
[10] Ibid.

10. Inside the Kremlin

Olga Oliker

For Russia's neighbors in the South Caucasus and Central Asia, the Ukraine crisis is a watershed moment. Since independence, these countries had pursued a "multi-vector" foreign policy, which meant seeking new partnerships while acknowledging their dependence on Russia and being careful to respect Russian red lines.

After the annexation of Crimea and destabilization of eastern Ukraine, the location of those red lines no longer seems clear. The resulting uncertainty is forcing the leaders of the South Caucasus and Central Asian states to be more deferential to Moscow in the near term while accelerating these states' efforts to loosen and diversify their ties with Moscow. Time, especially the emergence of a new generation of leaders with no memories of the Soviet Union, will only accelerate this process.

Before the outbreak of protests on Kyiv's Maidan Nezalezhnosti [Independence Square] in September 2013, Ukraine's strategy for dealing with Russia was multi-vector as well. Economic and cultural ties with Russia remained strong, but the government, even under the allegedly pro-Russian President Viktor Yanukovych (whose political career the Kremlin aided), sought to develop diplomatic, trade, and investment ties with other partners. For Ukraine, that meant primarily the European Union, while the South Caucasus and Central Asian states have looked variously to the United States, EU, Turkey, China, and elsewhere.

While these states pursued economic ties with a range of neigh-bors, they understood that Moscow regarded security cooperation, especially the presence of NATO or U.S. forces, as a red line, and steered clear—or paid the price. Georgia's courting of NATO, which contributed to the 2008 war with Russia, and Kyrgyzstan's hosting of U.S. forces at the Manas Transit Center, which helped fuel Moscow's role in ousting former President Kurmanbek Bakiyev, served as object lessons of the costs of seeking outside security assurances. Still, the rule seemed to be: trade with whomever you want at least as long as you do not challenge Russia's preferred position such as in EU energy markets, but keep U.S. and NATO forces out.

In line with this understanding, before the Maidan protests, post-Soviet elites from other states were generally weary of joining the Russian-backed Eurasian Customs Union with Belarus and Kazakh-stan, or the planned Eurasian Economic Union. Despite the fact that Kazakh President Nursultan Nazarbayev first proposed the Eurasian Union in the 1990s, many Kazakh officials and businessmen opposed Putin's scheme, and even Nazarbayev took pains to emphasize that the planned body was solely an economic union.

Others, including Armenia, where more than 5,000 Russian troops are based, as well as Kyrgyzstan and Tajikistan, whose econo-mies are heavily dependent on remittances from Russia, demurred. Meanwhile, Ukraine, along with Armenia, Georgia, and Moldova, ne-gotiated association agreements with the EU that, when implement-ed, would radically transform their economic and administrative structures, weakening inherited links with Russia. Although Moscow opposed these agreements and encouraged its neighbors to join its customs union, these countries largely continued charting their own course, mostly evincing little interest in the customs union.

Nevertheless, in the run-up to the EU summit where Armenia, Georgia, Moldova, and Ukraine were set to formalize their associa-tion agreements, Russia began exerting enormous political and eco-nomic pressure. In September, Armenia abruptly announced it was shelving its association agreement and would join the customs union. Soon thereafter, Ukrainian President Yanukovych also buckled, following a secretive two-day visit to Moscow. Yanukovych's about-face sparked the protests that led to his downfall, Russia's occupation of Crimea, and the insurgency in eastern Ukraine. These events seemed at odds with the previously accepted rules of the game. Russia's military intervention in Ukraine was driven more by post-colonial disregard than any prospect of NATO forces on its border (indeed, it was the Russian intervention that led new President Petro Poroshenko to again seek Ukrainian NATO membership).

Moreover, to justify the intervention, Putin proclaimed a wide-ranging mandate to protect "compatriots," "Russians and Russian-speakers" throughout the former USSR. This formula gave Moscow a pretext to intervene in any of its former dependencies—including the Baltic states. Incautious remarks from Putin about Kazakhstan lacking historical legitimacy only exacerbated the sense of concern in the neighborhood that Russia had gone rogue.

The Ukraine crisis held another lesson for the former Soviet states as well, a lesson about the dangers of "people power." The "Maidan scenario"—a corrupt, ineffective government thrown out by its own people—represents the greatest fear of many post–Soviet leaders. The result, in at least some states, has been greater repression and less openness, even if these crackdowns make a Maidan more likely in the longer term.

In the near term, the twin fear of Moscow and the Maidan is working to Russia's advantage. Unlike the West, Russia will not object to crackdowns on domestic opposition, while joining the Eurasian Economic Union provides some insurance against Russian meddling (a *krysha*, or roof, in Russian criminal slang). In the past year, Armenia and Kyrgyzstan have applied to join the Eurasian Economic Union, while Azerbaijan and Georgia have increasingly hedged their pro-Western orientations. Further driving this tilt toward Moscow is the perception, widespread especially in Central Asia, that U.S. engagement in the region is declining with the withdrawal from Afghanistan.

Yet the post–Soviet states view Russia's decision to change the rules of the game as a threat to their sovereignty. The crisis in Ukraine has strained the bonds of affection tying these states to Russia. While they may have little choice but to join Russian-led multilateral bodies, these countries will work to ensure that these entities remain toothless, and will redouble their efforts to reduce their dependence on and vulnerability to Russia. Almost without exception, elites in the South Caucasus and Central Asia see greater U.S. engagement as vital to the sovereignty and independence of the region's states.

The irony is that, as Putin made clear in 2008, Russia does not view Ukraine, any more than the states of the South Caucasus and Central Asia, as a "real state." By forcing these countries to defend their independence, Moscow is compelling them to define themselves and their national interests, often in opposition to Russia. Russia's actions are breeding a new national identity and pride, which will be the surest guarantee of these countries' sovereignty over the longer term.

11. A NATO Strategy for the Eastern Flank
Jeffrey Rathke

The guiding Russia's 2014 annexation of Crimea and intervention in eastern Ukraine mark an end to the European post–Cold War security order—but only if the United States and Europe assent to it. The West has additional policy cards to play, and should do so with confidence. As the July 2016 NATO Summit in Warsaw approaches, it is time for NATO to adopt a longer-term strategy for its eastern flank that goes beyond the reactive while maintaining transatlantic unity behind a common set of goals, actions, and capabilities for the coming decade that will reinforce the security of eastern allies and promote stability for NATO's bordering countries.

The United States and Europe have mobilized politically, militarily, and economically since February 2014: adopting defense measures to raise NATO's readiness and imposing economic sanctions that have had an impact on the Russian economy (amplified by the decline in global oil prices and Russian economic mismanagement). But divisions in NATO remain: eastern allies focused on Russia, southern allies on instability in the Middle East and North Africa.

The United States must lead NATO in turning these initial responsive elements into a persistent NATO strategy for the east, enhancing allied military presence, demonstrating long-term resolve, bolstering NATO's capacity to deter new Russian threats, setting the direction of resource decisions and interoperable procurements, and sharing the burden equitably on both sides of the Atlantic. This strategy should be developed in full consultation with non-NATO partners Sweden and Finland, who share NATO's concerns about Russia's activity in and around the Baltic Sea region, and where government and public opinion are increasingly open to a closer relationship with the Alliance, including eventual NATO membership. This would give the strategy additional depth, while building practical cooperation on core security interests with two high-end partners who could make significant contributions now, and even greater ones in the future if they choose to pursue NATO membership.

Strengthening deterrence on the eastern flank is essential. While the Alliance as a whole enjoys conventional superiority over Russia, NATO's eastern allies face a huge imbalance of Russian forces—armor, artillery, and air forces—in the Russian Western Military District. This imbalance is magnified by Russia's dramatically expanded exercise activity, demonstrating a level of readiness and mobilization that NATO cannot match at large scale. The quality and depth of Russia's military forces remains questionable, but this could change: Russia already has made rapid advances in materiel and tactics since its 2008 invasion of Georgia, advances that have been on full display in Crimea and eastern Ukraine.

U.S. engagement is central to sustaining NATO solidarity as a whole. The Obama administration's 12-month European Reassurance Initiative was crucial in securing additional NATO commitments, increasing deployments of fighter aircraft to Lithuania, Latvia, and Estonia to include F-22s, committing forces to the "spearhead" force (with its 48-hour response time), and establishing NATO command-and-control elements in the Baltic countries, Poland, Romania, and Bulgaria. A U.S. commitment of one battalion to the Baltic countries (in addition to existing U.S. forces in Europe) could be part of an approach to leverage commitments from other allies to two additional battalion-sized units, constituting a Baltic brigade. A brigade-sized presence in the Baltic states, especially with participation from the United States and NATO's larger member states, would demonstrate shared resolve across the Alliance, raising a significant hurdle to Russian attempts at coercion or destabilization.

Some NATO allies may seek to reopen the debate from 2014 about whether the presence of allied forces in its easternmost territories should be described as "permanent" rather than "persistent." Permanent presence was resisted by some allies, particularly Germany, which wanted to avoid contradicting the 1997 NATO-Russia Founding Act's language that NATO would not permanently station substantial combat forces on the territory of its new eastern members "in the current and foreseeable security environment." NATO papered over the issue at the Wales Summit by describing NATO's presence as "continuous . . . on a rotating basis." NATO should avoid an internal battle over declaring the Founding Act null and void; it is in practice, anyway. Allies should instead focus on signals that its adversary will understand: that in the current and foreseeable security environment, NATO's presence in the east will be continuous and will grow.

The development of a sustained NATO presence along its eastern flank will require greater investment in defense, and greater readiness and ability to deploy forces. The majority of NATO allies (17 of 28) have begun to increase defense spending in real terms, a hopeful sign. But spending by four of the five allies with the largest defense budgets continues to decline in real terms (the UK, France, Germany, and Italy). Among numbers 6 through 10, only Turkey, Poland, and the Netherlands show more than marginal increases in spending. The vast majority of NATO members still fall well below the Wales Summit target of spending 2 percent of GDP on defense. By other measures such as research and development and major equipment spending, allies also are well short of their goals. It will be crucial at the NATO summit for allies to demonstrate that they are putting meaningful resources behind their commitments, through a combination of increased national spending and NATO commonly-funded infrastructure.

In preparation for the Warsaw Summit, the United States should make clear that it is prepared to put the necessary forces, alongside other NATO allies, on NATO's eastern flank to deter potential Russian destabilizing efforts for the long term, not simply send forces to reassure. This will entail making difficult strategic choices, but it will send a clear signal to NATO allies, Russia, and NATO's neighbors that America will lead.

12. Sino-Russian Cooperation

Jeffrey Mankoff

Beginning with Richard Nixon's 1973 visit to China, balancing between Moscow and Beijing has been a centerpiece of U.S. foreign policy. Today, though, Washington's relations with both Beijing and Moscow are difficult, while China and Russia increasingly cooperate in the economic, military, and political spheres. How durable is today's Sino-Russian cooperation, and how worried should the United States be?

In many ways, Sino-Russian cooperation results from a natural complementarity of interests, and long predates the current period of tension with the United States. Yet growing estrangement from the United States is pushing Moscow and Beijing to deepen their cooperation in other, more troubling areas. The two countries nonetheless remain at odds in much of their shared region, while Russia needs China much more than China needs it. While China and Russia are united in opposing a global order dominated by Washington, the positive agenda of these large, self-interested powers is murkier. The United States still has an opportunity to exploit their differences, if it can avoid driving them closer first.

China and Russia are complementary in many ways. Russia's massive reserves of natural resources have a natural market in China, while Chinese investment capital helps Russia develop these resources. Trade turnover grew from just $4.4 billion in 1992 to $89 billion in 2013, and China has been Russia's largest individual trade partner since 2010. Then-presidents Hu Jintao and Dmitry Medve-dev announced in 2011 that bilateral trade turnover would reach $100 billion in 2015, and $200 billion by 2020.

After more than a decade of negotiations, Moscow and Beijing signed a massive $400 billion gas deal in the spring of 2014, aim-ing to bring 38 billion cubic meters (bcm) a year of gas from Eastern Siberia to China through the newly built Power of Siberia pipeline. A subsequent framework agreement called for an additional 10 bcm via the so-called Altai pipeline.

Beyond economic cooperation, Moscow and Beijing have simi-lar political cultures and a worldview emphasizing states' absolute sovereignty while condemning U.S. military-political intervention to change regimes abroad. Fearing that the United States views re-gime change in Moscow and Beijing as its ultimate goal, Russia and China provide mutual support for efforts to clamp down on the media and civil society. They oppose Washington's efforts to overthrow repressive governments, for instance in Syria. Russia also plays a critical role in China's ongoing military moderniza-tion, selling advanced cruise missiles, radars, and other technol-ogy that supports Beijing's anti-access/area denial strategy in the Western Pacific.

China and Russia also support the establishment of a new eco-nomic and security architecture to reduce the centrality of the United States to the international system. Seeking to reduce the role of the dollar in international transactions, Moscow and Beijing agreed in 2010 to trade their currencies against one another, while earlier this year they agreed to settle bilateral trade in rubles and yuan, rather than dollars. Washington's threats to bar Russia from the SWIFT (Society for Worldwide Interbank Financial Transaction) system prompted Moscow and Beijing to discuss an alternative payment mechanism to circumvent sanctions.

China and Russia are also driving efforts to establish new mul-tilateral forums that give them a greater say in writing the rules of twenty-first-century international cooperation. With Washington unwilling to overhaul representation in the Bretton Woods institutions, China in particular spearheaded the creation of alternative financial institutions, including the Asian Infrastructure Investment Bank and the BRICS (Brazil, Russia, India, China, South Africa) New Development Bank. On the security side, Moscow and Beijing are the driving forces behind the Shanghai Cooperation Organization (SCO). While largely an umbrella for bilateral deals, the SCO also facilitates information sharing about dissidents along with joint exercises among member states' militaries.

Though Central Asia has long been an arena for Sino-Russian competition, in recent years Beijing and Moscow have emphasized cooperative approaches. Russia's planned Eurasian Economic Union (EEU) in part seeks to limit the penetration of Chinese goods into Central Asia, while the Silk Road Economic Belt (SREB) that Xi Jinping unveiled in late 2013 aims to create a new transportation corridor to Europe via Central Asia that largely bypasses Russia. Yet last May, Xi and Putin agreed to combine the two initiatives, with China agreeing to build an additional rail corridor through Russia.

Although economic and security cooperation has accelerated in recent years as both Moscow and Beijing have endured periods of greater tension with the United States, their relationship remains plagued by mistrust and constrained by Sino-Russian asymmetries. Slower growth in China has curbed Beijing's appetite for Russian hydrocarbons, while lower global energy prices have made projects like Power of Siberia less economical, leading to delays. Bilateral trade has fallen short of the goals set by Hu and Medvedev; total trade is likely to decline by nearly a third in 2015, while investment fell by a fifth in the first seven months of the year. Currency deals have suffered from the ruble's volatility.

Rather than express solidarity against Western sanctions, China has taken advantage of Russia's isolation. Beijing refused the $25 billion prepayment Moscow sought to start construction on Power of Siberia and suspended the Altai pipeline, which it never wanted in the first place. State-owned Chinese companies successfully demanded equity stakes in Russian oil and gas fields, which the Kremlin steadfastly refused to grant to private Western firms.

Russia and China may share an aversion to democracy promotion, but they apply their commitment to sovereignty in different ways. Beijing simultaneously opposed the ouster of Viktor Yanukovych and Russia's promotion of separatism in Crimea and the Donbas (which Beijing viewed as a potential precedent for foreign intervention in Tibet or Xinjiang). China views sovereignty in absolute terms, while Russia wants the right to intervene in its neighbors without the assent of their governments.

Despite their declared ambition to integrate the EEU and the Silk Road Economic Belt, the underlying logic of the two projects still differs. New rail lines across Russia will compete with the transportation corridors China is building in Central Asia, benefiting Chinese shippers most of all. In any case, many of the Central Asian states see the EEU as a neo-imperial endeavor and look to China (and the United States) as a counterweight against Russian influence.

Elsewhere, Russia's efforts to expand its arms sales to partners including India and Vietnam are at odds with Chinese ambitions to regional primacy. Moscow refuses to speak out on China's maritime territorial disputes (while selling advanced submarines to Vietnam), and has made efforts to improve relations with Japan.

The Sino-Russian partnership is more than an axis of convenience, but far less than an alliance. China and Russia remain major powers that prioritize self-interest over any shared vision of the future. Each is a revisionist power in its own way, and at the global level, discomfort with the status quo is the main adhesive in their partnership.

U.S. policy is thus a major variable that will determine the future of Sino-Russian cooperation. Today, opposition to what both see as U.S. containment and democracy promotion accelerates their cooperation. The United States has reasons for pushing back against Russian actions in Ukraine, Chinese territorial claims, cyber espionage, and other affronts. Yet it cannot simply and permanently write off either Russia or China. Containment has to be tempered with engagement; Russia and China are simply too big and powerful to isolate at the same time.

PART V

Northeast, Southeast, and South Asia

13. Reform Cold, Politics Hot: President Xi Jinping at Mid-Term

Christopher K. Johnson

Around the turn of this century, analysts of Sino-Japanese relations began characterizing the relationship between East Asia's two biggest powers with the simple shorthand "Politics Cold, Economics Hot" to explain the awkward circumstances in which issues related to Japan's wartime history strained the two countries' political ties while substantial Japanese investment in China's booming economy kept bilateral trade humming along. Although the description did not fully capture the complexities of the China-Japan relationship, it provided a framework for explaining the seemingly contradictory impulses underpinning the interactions between Tokyo and Beijing during that period. As President and Chinese Communist Party (CCP) General Secretary Xi Jinping passes the effective midpoint in his first five-year term in office, a similar juxtaposition may offer some explanatory power in thinking about the equally incongruous relationship between the ostensible slowdown in momentum behind Xi's bold reform vision unveiled at the watershed Third Plenum of the 18th Central Committee in November 2013, and what appears to be his political resilience in the face of passive resistance to his agenda from CCP elites, economic volatility at home, and an increasingly complex geopolitical landscape abroad. In a phrase, then, China's current domestic political dynamic can perhaps best be described as "Reform Cold, Politics Hot."

There is little doubt the leadership seems to have stepped at least somewhat off of the reform pathway hinted at in the heady days following the Third Plenum. Several factors are believed to have contributed to this development. First and foremost, President Xi has seemingly adopted a more cautious approach in recent months as China's economic slowdown has worsened. The volatility brought on by the steep drop in China's equity markets and a ham-handed effort to devalue the Chinese currency have only served to reinforce the president's natural statist tendencies. And therein lies the point—these are Xi's instincts and predilections, and not, as is frequently postulated in Western press accounts and academic writings, a continuing manifestation of China's "fragmented authoritarianism," or the notion that Chinese leaders simply cannot fail to overcome—or even constrain—the system's many vested interests.

Instead, some observers view the leadership's seemingly more orthodox approach as an indication that President Xi is essentially a "fair-weather reformer." In other words, when the economy's prospects appear bright, it is easy for Xi to talk up and endorse reform, but, when the system confronts the pressures of a sustained economic downturn and the messiness associated with persistent economic volatility—much of which is rooted in the pursuit of reform itself—Xi's, and the CCP system's, instincts for intervention and control win out.

But to suggest that the party chief is easily blown off course by the changing winds of economic circumstances is too simplistic and is to deny Xi's serious commitment to a leading role for the state in China's economic future. Xi's approach in this regard is well in line with 30 years of CCP practice of viewing increased marketization of the economy as a means to refine state-owned enterprises (SOEs) in the fires of competition rather than putting the economy on a path toward eventual privatization. Against this backdrop, President Xi's developing vision for transitioning the definition of what constitutes a successful SOE away from the current model of domestically focused industrial giants toward the nimble, globally competitive national champions that his policies seek to cultivate represents what the leadership's propagandists would define as "a new theoretical breakthrough" in further refining China's unique model of state capitalism.

So, if this is what Xi wants, and he is arguably the most powerful Chinese leader in more than two decades, then what is the problem? Put simply, Xi likely would characterize the relatively slow progress to date on advancing the Third Plenum reforms as a "Human Resources" problem, or passive resistance from officials in senior positions who are holdovers associated with his two immediate predecessors, former Presidents Hu Jintao and Jiang Zemin. Judging from their persistent calls in official media for pushing ahead more aggressively on reforms, China's most ardently reform economists worry that this assessment means that Xi is putting most of his energy into managing the leadership reshuffle that will accompany the 19th Party Congress in 2017 at the very time they need him to be visibly and personally championing progress on the reforms.

But Xi would argue that his intense focus on the politics is entirely justified. The investigations into the several "tigers"—regime code for high-level officials—netted thus far in Xi's anticorruption drive variously revealed that individuals in charge of the security services, the military, and even the Politburo's nerve center were pursuing agendas independent of those of the CCP's top leadership—a particularly unsettling state of affairs for a stove-piped Leninist bureaucracy riding atop a dynamic and diverse society. Moreover, despite Xi's various efforts to short-circuit the CCP's existing mechanisms for formulating policy—whether it be the anticorruption drive or the creation of new and powerful party decision making bodies responsive to him—the fact remains that, at the end of the day, he still is confronted with a Politburo that he had very little hand in shaping.

At the same time, if the leadership in 2017 follows the norms that have governed leadership reshuffles at the last several party congresses, most of the officials poised to rise to the apex of the CCP policymaking system are allies of Hu Jintao. As the scion of one of the founding fathers of the regime and therefore a very traditional Chinese leader, Xi intuitively understands that he must run the table at the 19th Party Congress to firm up his grip on the regime's key levers of power. Still, Xi cannot completely disregard the patterns of promotion that have developed over the last two decades in which certain criteria—such as service in a mixture of provincial and ministerial posts or experience in the CCP's central bureaucracy—are required for advancement, or, at a minimum, can serve as a way for senior party barons to object to the elevation of their rivals' handpicked supporters.

So where does this leave China's domestic politics going forward? Volatility and uncertainty are likely to remain the watchwords well into next year as the political situation remains unsettled. The recently concluded Fifth Plenum of the 18th Central Committee made no senior personnel announcements that might clarify the direction of the regime's high politics. The black box of CCP leadership wrangling makes it impossible to know whether Xi sought major changes or not, but the fact remains that the absence of movement represents a missed opportunity to signal to the bureaucracy a clear political bearing. Given Xi's likely belief that controlling personnel assignments in the runup to the 19th Party Congress is critical to the rest of his agenda, stasis on that front may further distract Xi's attention from pushing forward reform. In fact, the continued inertia could prompt Xi to consider more dramatic moves, such as further takedowns of retired or sitting senior leaders under the anticorruption drive, a more pointed assault on the party bureaucracy, or an effort to stage a bold demonstration of his political power. Such uncertainty, and its possible attendant leadership discord, would only serve to exacerbate doubts in the global community about the leadership's commitment to prioritizing the economy coming off the turbulence and volatility of recent months.

14. Economic Consequences of China's Slowdown

Scott Kennedy

Perhaps the most popular term used among strategic analysts in the past year is "Thucydides Trap"—the notion that a rising power and the incumbent power are destined for war—because of the growing rivalry between the United States and China. The worry is that as China's economy continues to grow, China will gain the means and confidence to challenge American military primacy and influence in Asia. From this perspective, China's recent economic slowdown is viewed as helpful in putting off the day of reckoning.

While perhaps comforting to some, there is more to fear from China's current economic weakness than its potential future strength. The empirical evidence about strategic rivalry is actually much more ambiguous than some prognosticators insist. And in the Chinese case, although anxieties have risen because of tensions over China's irredentist ambitions in the South China Sea and cyber, open warfare over these issues seems highly unlikely or unnecessary. Even more important, the negative consequences to the world—which must include both China and other countries—from its economic weakness are not just hypothetical; they are already visible and could become more damaging if not addressed soon.

China avoided the worst of the global financial crisis with an RMB 4 trillion stimulus package. But that binge in infrastructure spending has been followed by a hangover of debt and overcapacity. Domestic demand for electricity, steel, cement, copper, and glass has all fallen off, as have imports and exports. The only thing keeping the country out of recession is resilient employment and consumption data, accompanied by a gradual transition toward services, which is less dependent on infrastructure growth. The International Monetary Fund estimates GDP growth will be 6.8 percent for 2015 and 6.3 percent for 2016. Chinese authorities dispute these figures, but most other independent estimates are even lower. Slower growth would be acceptable if achieved through greater efficiency and higher productivity, but unfortunately, what China calls the "new normal" looks a lot like the old normal, just slower.

Concern about China's poor economic performance is not only the result of built-up debt, but recent policy swings. Xi Jinping came into power advertising a comprehensive reform package. He started with a range of reforms in finance, utility prices, fiscal affairs, and free-trade zones, but in the past year, we've seen a string of policy moves that are decidedly more statist. Having placed constraints on the real estate sector in 2013, authorities in 2014 encouraged investment in the stock market, and then when the expected bubble burst in 2015, they intervened to slow the collapse, suspending trading of many stocks, ordering shareholders not to sell, and reportedly using $500 billion to soak up unwanted shares. The Shanghai Index fell off over 40 percent, and trading volume fell over 70 percent. The stock market fiasco was followed in August by the poorly managed liberalization of the renminbi, which has featured an extended tussle between the market and authorities over the RMB's value, with the former expecting further depreciation. While authorities spent billions to maintain the RMB's strength, Chinese citizens simultaneously shipped their dollars out of the country at record pace, leading to a decline in foreign exchange holdings.

The mistakes of the summer were accompanied by cheap-calorie stimulus, with several cuts in lending rates, ramped-up fiscal spending, and an RMB 3.6 trillion debt-swap program involving local government bonds. The reform package for state-owned enterprises (SOEs) announced in September 2015 highlighted strengthened party control, mergers, minority private investment, and limited competition. And signs emerged that the 13th Five-Year Plan (2016–2020) would bring only incremental liberalization.

Slower growth and greater volatility in the short term mean a rise in debt and corporate losses, which may very well translate into higher unemployment and a slowdown in household consumption. And given the unpredictable mix of market and state in recent policies, doubts are growing about the leadership's basic competence to govern the economy, which had always been the Communist Party's strong suit.

From the perspective of the United States and others, slower Chinese growth means less demand for their goods. Commodity prices have fallen off, hurting Australia, Brazil, and the Middle East. And exports to China of manufactured intermediate goods and final products from the United States, Europe, and other industrialized economies have all dropped. American exports to China are estimated to fall by at least 9 percent in 2015, and could fall by a larger amount in 2016 if China's economy continues to lag. A more slowly growing pie could also translate into greater protectionism, a trend already visible in high-tech goods such as semiconductors and telecommunications.

But the most important emerging negative externalities from China's economic troubles are volatility in global securities markets and greater pressure on macroeconomic policies for the United States and others. China's economy is now large enough and its capital markets open enough that problems there spread elsewhere at the speed of light, as investors everywhere move their funds with just the click of a button.

The most pressing challenge then is not faster growth, but more unambiguously market-oriented economic policies that are also more clearly articulated and explained. It is in China's strong self-interest to calm markets and restore the confidence of investors, domestic and global. Even if further stimulus is warranted, accompanying it with greater liberalization and market access, for example in services, would be an important signal that Xi Jinping is not just a fair-weather reformer.

At the same time, the United States can emphasize even further the benefits to China and to the bilateral relationship of China pursuing an unambiguous reform policy agenda. The conclusion and implementation of the Trans-Pacific Partnership (TPP) would also serve as bright directional arrows pointing China to further open its economy, as remaining outside TPP would put China's economy at a strategic disadvantage precisely in those high-value-added sectors in which it is hoping to develop greater capacity. Finally, China's hosting of the G-20 process in 2016 provides another opportunity to strengthen coordination of macroeconomic policies and further hone strategies toward healthier and broad-based growth strategies.

Generating better economic performance in China should be welcomed, not feared. A potential Thucydides Trap is hypothetical, whereas the negative consequences from China falling into a "middle-income trap" are real and potentially upon us.

15. Geopolitical Consequences of China's Slowdown

Bonnie S. Glaser and Matthew Funaiole

Despite being widely recognized as the most powerful emerging country in the world, China's international position rests upon an untested foundation. Unlike other leading countries, whose national strength emanates from the confluence of military, economic, social, and geopolitical vectors, Chinese power is inexorably tied to the expansion of the Chinese economy. Breakneck economic growth has greatly elevated China's regional standing, but Beijing's goal of becoming a regional leader—which may eventually extend to displacing American preeminence in the Asia-Pacific—has yet to be achieved.

The halcyon days of China's unbridled economic growth are coming to an end. Growth rates have dropped, weaknesses in the Chinese stock market have been exposed, and China's aging workforce poses a serious demographic challenge. Notwithstanding these problems, the Chinese economy remains the primary source of China's national power, and the leadership is wrestling with how to translate the nation's economic clout into increased influence, especially in Asia.

Chinese President Xi Jinping's top foreign policy priority is to persuade China's neighbors that China is a benign leader that can be trusted to assume the reigns of a new Sino-centric regional order. Xi's vision of "Asia for Asians" foresees a greater role for China within the region, but with economic strength serving as the primary driver of China's resurgence, China lacks the leverage to fundamentally alter the U.S.-dominated regional order. Countries in the Asia-Pacific are keen to reap economic benefits from China's rapid rise, but desire a strong U.S. presence to serve as a counterweight to the uncertainty created by growing Chinese power.

As leaders in Beijing endeavor to bolster China's regional position, they face an uphill battle mitigating negative perceptions of China while simultaneously expanding Chinese influence. The most direct means for an emerging power to reaffirm its international position is through enhancing its military strength. Although economic growth has fueled the expansion of Chinese military capabilities, Beijing must still rely upon its economic power to weaken American influence and promote Chinese interests. Reverting to outright military force or coercion would be counterproductive: it would entice China's neighbors to band together with the United States in an anti-China coalition. Consequently, Chinese leaders must temper Chinese short-term military power projection so as to not compromise the perception they are cultivating of China as a benign regional hegemon.

In an effort to counter American influence without directly challenging U.S. hegemony, Chinese leaders have embarked on an ambitious strategy to expand Chinese interests through the establishment of new financial institutions. Xi has actively pushed his regional economic agenda through the creation of the Asian Infrastructure Investment Bank (AIIB), which supports a Chinese-style infrastructure development framework for the broader Asia-Pacific region. By design, the AIIB will rival predominately U.S.-dominated financial institutions, such as the International Monetary Fund and the World Bank.

It's not difficult to see why China would back such initiatives. Institutions like the IMF have been routinely criticized for giving preference to the development agendas of the United States and Western Europe. Cultivating new institutional linkages across Asia offers China a means to address its concerns with the prevailing U.S.-centric security arrangements that dominate the region by rewarding the countries that acquiesce to Chinese interests in return for economic advantages, development assistance, and technological benefits. These arrangements harken back to the ancient tributary system, through which China exacted compliance from neighboring states on matters of politics, defense, and economics.

Nowhere is this Chinese alternative to the U.S. hub-and-spoke network more evident than with China's most ambitious development project—One Belt, One Road (OBOR). OBOR seeks to connect China's economy with infrastructure networks across Eurasia and into the Middle East. By fostering collaboration across the historic Silk Road and developing a new maritime branch, Chinese leaders are actively pursuing strategic initiatives designed to redirect the global economy to run through Asia, along corridors that lead to Beijing.

In their efforts to establish a Chinese-centered hierarchical order, Chinese leaders have embarked on an ambitious, yet risky strategy. The AIIB and OBOR are subsidized by the Chinese economy. While supported by numerous countries besides China, it is unlikely that either project will succeed without Chinese economic backing. In this way, Chinese leaders are attempting to expand China's regional influence by doubling down on economic power.

Overinvestment in economic initiatives leaves Beijing susceptible to the same vulnerabilities that threaten the Chinese economy. Should the Chinese economy stumble, aspects of the AIIB and OBOR will need to be scaled back. The knock-on effects of an economic slowdown could diminish China's future role in the region. The smaller countries of Asia have tolerated Chinese assertiveness in exchange for economic gains and because they fear that challenging China could cause Beijing to punish them economically. If China is no longer able to afford those benefits, many smaller countries may be less willing to show deference and more willing to push back against Chinese threats to their interests.

In the South China Sea, where in recent years China has incrementally altered the status quo in its favor, such a development could have a positive effect. Myriad steps taken by some of the other claimants to the disputed land features, as well as by the United States, Japan, and other concerned members of the international community, have not persuaded Beijing to moderate its assertiveness and seek cooperative solutions to the extant territorial disputes.

Any reduction in Chinese influence may diminish the disincentives that smaller claimant states and the Association of Southeast Asian Nations (ASEAN) face vis-à-vis China. Firmer and coordinated policies among Vietnam, the Philippines, and Malaysia, combined with greater unity among all the ASEAN member countries, might induce Beijing to conclude a binding code of conduct for the South China Sea that ensures disputes are managed peacefully and in accordance with international law.

Similarly, China's economic slowdown could offer Japan an occasion to gain leverage in the Sino-Japanese relationship, creating the possibility to tamp down tensions in the East China Sea and stabilize bilateral ties that remain a fragile, but critically important, component of the regional security landscape. Perhaps most significantly, a Chinese economic slowdown affords the United States an opportunity to buttress its political, economic, and military position in the Asia-Pacific, and assuage worries that the United States lacks sufficient strategic vision and political commitment to the region. The outcome relies on how Washington plays its hand, but the result could be the strengthening of a rules-based, U.S.-led security architecture in the Asia-Pacific region for years to come.

16. Beyond TTP: Shaping an Economic Strategy in Asia

Ernest Z. Bower, Matthew P. Goodman, and Scott Miller

Few things are as important for America's future as an effective international economic policy. The United States urgently needs a comprehensive economic strategy toward the Asia-Pacific, a region that will do more to determine U.S. interests over coming decades than any other.

America is a Pacific power, and our prosperity and security are inextricably linked to Asia's. The region is home to the world's three largest economies—the United States, China, and Japan—and 8 of the world's 15 countries with gross domestic product of over $1 trillion a year. More than 60 percent of Fortune Global 500 companies are headquartered in the Asia-Pacific. But the facts on the ground in Asia are fundamentally changing. By 2030, the region will be home to two-thirds of the world's middle class. Most of the growth will take place in China and India, which are returning to their traditional positions at the center of Asian economic and political affairs.

Achieving the United States' broader political and security goals in Asia depends on sustained economic engagement. Our allies and close partners there want the United States to be deeply engaged in the region, but many question our staying power. They believe that an active U.S. economic role in the region will not only enhance our shared prosperity but also sustain an enduring and mutually beneficial U.S. security role. Asians also see engagement with our leading firms and supplying our consumers as vital to their growth and national security. Most of all, they need U.S. initiative to help shape the region's economic rules and norms.

With Trade Promotion Authority in hand, the next task is to ratify the Trans-Pacific Partnership (TPP), a comprehensive trade agreement that will deepen integration among 12 economies across the Pacific and boost U.S. exports and growth. Success of the TPP and continued growth at home will show that the United States can still be the kind of economic leader that others want to follow.

Then what? The immediate question will be how to take the TPP forward. Several other Asian partners—South Korea, the Philippines, and Taiwan—have expressed keen interest in joining the TPP. Developing creative new approaches for engaging other key economies—including China, Indonesia, and India, three of the world's largest countries—in bilateral and multilateral arrangements over time is critical. Much of this work will fall to the next administration that will take office in January 2017.

More broadly, the next U.S. administration will need to articulate a comprehensive economic strategy for the Asia-Pacific region, covering not only trade and investment but also finance, development, energy, and all other dimensions of U.S. economic engagement. The new vision must encompass all of Asia's major economies and recognize the fundamental linkage to U.S. geopolitical strategy in the region.

The overarching goal of the new strategy should be to advance U.S. prosperity and security by promoting an open and fair trans-Pacific economic order, built on rule of law, market-based competition, and sustainability. This will help reinforce existing U.S. advantages as a leader in innovation and entrepreneurship, promote the interests of all Americans through enhanced economic opportunities, and embed us in a region of 8 billion future consumers, innovators, and entrepreneurs.

Central to our strategy must be establishing a productive and realistic relationship with China. Today, Beijing is asserting its regional interests in a way unprecedented in the modern era, from building islands in the South China Sea to pursuing a vigorous economic diplomacy under the "One Belt, One Road" strategy. We must seek a shared vision of peace and prosperity with China, challenge Beijing when it strays from international norms, and sharpen our will to compete economically. We also must understand the perspective of other nations in the region, from treaty allies to India to the Association of Southeast Asian Nations (ASEAN) and Pacific Island economies, and partner with them to promote prosperity.

To carry out the strategy, adequate resources—funding, policy-making attention, and political capital—will need to be mobilized. This in turn means our political leaders need to be willing to talk more to the American people about Asia, our position as a Pacific power, and the fundamental role the region plays in all of our lives economically and politically.

Asia's impressive economic rise and overall political stability have enabled Washington policymakers to take the region for granted, as we have been busy coping with crises in Europe, the Middle East, and elsewhere. Our long-term economic and security stakes in the Asia-Pacific demand that this critical region capture more "space of mind" among policymakers and the American people alike.

17. Interested in India's Geopolitical Future? Look to Its States

Richard M. Rossow

For years, India-watchers have by equal measure championed the nation's future role as the next regional if not global power and bemoaned its failure to live up to its strategic potential. At the heart of this optimism has been India's fundamental capacities and characteristics—the size of its population, its democratic system of government, its geographic location in the heart of a dynamic Asia, and its deep and talented human capital pool. And yet, the pessimism has derived from the seeming inability of the federal government to make the whole equal more than the sum of its parts. While there are many reasons for this dichotomy, one of the most important is the outsized role played by India's states in policymaking. To predict India's future course, one must have a better understanding of its composite states.

In 2016, four Indian states and one territory with a combined population of nearly 230 million will hold elections.[1] The list includes Assam, Kerala, Tamil Nadu, West Bengal, and the union territory of Puducherry. These elections are important for India's economic development for three reasons. First, state governments collectively have a larger impact on India's growth than the central government. Second, the strength of key regional parties has allowed them to manipulate federal legislative reforms. And third, the BJP is not expect-

[1] Election Commission of India, "Terms of the Houses," http://bit.ly/1g1oFNx.

ed to be a major player in most of these elections, providing a cushion against the pain that some of India's more important reforms may cause in the short term, such as reducing subsidies. For political junkies, there is another intriguing reason to follow these elections: to see if the Congress Party can begin to reverse its electoral losing streak, as two of the states holding elections are held by Congress.

The Seventh Schedule to India's Constitution establishes the distribution of power within India's federal system: it provides three different lists of subjects and articulates which agencies have the power to govern on these issues. Some subjects fall under the purview of states, others the central government, and a third list falls under the "concurrent list" that can be either the center's or states'. State leaders have nearly complete authority over critical elements of their economies such as power distribution, water distribution, law and order, land acquisition, and a wide range of business permits.

There is now heightened interest in state-level developments in India considering the Modi government's goal of increasing competition among states for business. In September 2015, the Department of Industrial Policy and Promotion (DIPP) released its initial findings[2] of a broad study measuring the ease of doing business in Indian states, providing India's first "apples to apples" overview of the states. India's ability to reach double-digit, sustained growth will ultimately be a reflection of the larger states' enacting pro-growth policies, and will ultimately be a critical factor in whether India embraces broader trade liberalization in the future. One helpful, if imperfect, indicator of the differences between states is to review India's per capita income levels.[3] For fiscal year 2014, per capita income levels range from Rs. 15,506 (a bit under $500) in Bihar, up to Rs. 224,138 (around $3,500) in Goa.

The strength and influence of India's regional parties on the central government's ability to take legislative decisions cannot be overstated. Looking at the states holding elections in 2016, the parties that

[2] World Bank,, "Assessment of State Implementation of Business Rules," September 2015, http://bit.ly/1NrvBUn

[3] Niti Aayog (National Institution for Transforming India), "Per Capita NSDP at Current Prices (2004-05 to 2014-15), http://bit.ly/1inGLoL.

currently run West Bengal and Tamil Nadu, the Trinamool Congress and AIADMK respectively, hold the third and fourth most seats in the lower house of India's national Parliament. Both also rank among the six largest parties in the upper house of Parliament. As we have seen from past Parliament sessions, opponents to specific bills do not need huge numbers to block legislative reforms. The connection between these state elections and federal reforms is most apparent when you consider that the upper house of Parliament is indirectly elected by India's state legislatures. The BJP currently controls less than 20 percent of seats in the upper house. Regional parties hold around half of the upper house seats, and this block is unlikely to change dramatically for several years, even if the BJP continues winning state elections.

India's 2016 state elections also provide a bit of respite for the BJP in balancing federal reforms and local political concerns. Of the five elections, Assam is the only state in which the BJP has a reasonable chance of coming to power. So short-term political considerations should not weigh so heavily on the party's desire to enact reforms that may create immediate discomfort to voters. Some of the Modi government's priority legislative reforms, including land acquisition and labor reforms, are already generating real political heat. But relaxing burdensome rules governing these crucial business factors is frequently listed as among the most important economic reforms to stimulate growth.

Finally, the state elections in 2016 will provide another opportunity to measure if the Congress Party remains in free-fall, or if they can begin holding ground. Two states holding elections next year, Assam and Kerala, are among the most populous states where Congress remains in power. Winning reelection in Kerala is already a difficult challenge based on electoral precedence; the state has not re-elected a sitting government in more than thirty years.

There is a growing appreciation of the importance of the political economies of Indian states when trying to develop a deeper picture of India's national trajectory. Much like the United States, it seems there is always another election around the corner. State leaders play a crucial role in determining the success of India's hopes for economic growth. Regional parties can either play a supportive role, or a spoiler role in the Modi government's legislative reform plans. But perhaps the most important way to look at next year's state elections is the contrast between what these elections mean for India's two main national parties. The BJP has relatively little chance of coming to power in all but one of these states, potentially allowing the Modi government to take some politically difficult decisions. On the other hand, the Congress Party will be fighting to remain a genuine political force in India.

This political battle at the state level will do much to determine what type of India emerges geopolitically in Asia and on the global stage.

18. North Korean Vulnerability

Victor Cha and Lisa Collins

Tensions between North and South Korea escalated rapidly in the late summer of 2015 after an August 4 landmine blast in the demilitarized zone (DMZ), the fortified border that separates the two sides of the peninsula. The explosion blew off the legs of two patrolling South Korean soldiers and triggered a heated exchange between the two sides. After an 11-year hiatus, South Korea began broadcasting propaganda on loudspeakers along the border toward the North. Pyongyang promptly fired on the speakers, declaring it was entering "semi-war" status, which prompted a return of fire from the ROK.

The crisis was diffused after the announcement of an inter-Korean accord reached on August 25. The agreement, in which Pyongyang consented to end its semi-war status in exchange for a promise from Seoul to stop broadcasting propaganda, followed 43 hours of negotiations between the two Koreas. Are we likely to see more of these crises in 2016?

The two Koreas have clashed along the DMZ many times since the signing of the 1953 armistice. But this latest series of events is striking in at least one way. The most telling aspect of the 2015 crisis is how it offered insights into North Korean fragility. Contrary to popular opinion, Seoul's desire to stem the downturn in the country's stock exchange, and other untoward effects of North Korean saber-rattling on capital outflows, did not stop the crisis. Nor did the U.S. decision to temporarily halt military exercises with South Korea that were taking place in mid-August. The key to defusing the tense situation was actually Pyongyang's desire to stop the South Korean loudspeaker broadcasts. To accomplish this, the regime took the unusual step of acknowledging the August 4 landmine blast.

The North has not offered similar statements of regret over actions in the past, including the March 2010 sinking of the warship the Cheonan, which killed 46 South Korean soldiers, or the November 2010 shelling of Yeonpyeong Island, which killed four South Koreans. The inter-Korean agreement is even more striking because North Korea took a deal without having its demand met for a cessation of the U.S.-South Korean exercises.

Before the crisis abated, the North issued an unusual ultimatum directly to South Korean national security adviser Kim Kwan-jin, threatening to attack not in response to U.S.-ROK military exercises, but if the speakers were not silenced. Propaganda broadcasting had been a staple of the two Koreas' psychological warfare during the Cold War. But the new broadcasts were different from the knee-jerk anti-North Korean government propaganda of the Cold War. The recent broadcasts featured young females, who identified themselves as defectors, criticizing the Kim regime for its poor governance, human rights abuses, and isolation.

A recent broadcast segment featured a well-known North Korean journalist-turned-defector, Ju Seong-ha, who mocked photos of the rotund Kim's getting off planes like an exalted state guest. Sweet voices carrying powerful messages from 11 locations along the DMZ penetrated the minds of young, undernourished, and overworked North Korean soldiers. With better technology than the Cold War days, these broadcasts went deeper than before, blasting messages—and sometimes K-Pop music—more than a dozen miles into the country. This certainly rattled Pyongyang.

The normal North Korea playbook would have been to ratchet up tensions, play tough, have Kim visit military field units, draw missile strike lines to U.S. cities, and milk the crisis for as long as it can to get something—food, energy, a seat at the negotiating table with the United States. But this time, the sole issue was to stop the broadcasting.

This is not the first time North Korea has demonstrated such sensitivities. The U.N. Commission of Inquiry's Feb. 2014 recommendation to refer North Korea's leadership to the International Criminal Court (ICC) for crimes against humanity greatly disturbed North Korea, forcing them to do things they do not normally do. The regime sent its foreign minister Ri Su Yong to Russia for the first time in four years, and dispatched seasoned diplomat Kang Sok Ju to tour European capitals to lobby against the resolution. And finally, there was Pyongyang's apoplectic late 2014 rage in response to the movie The Interview that ridiculed the leadership, and that led to the North's cyber attack on Sony Pictures.

The lesson here is that the North Korean concession may mask a deeper vulnerability—and potentially larger crisis—down the road. Ultimately, the crisis demonstrates that the regime, under the 32- or 33-year-old Kim Jong-un, is vulnerable to attacks on its legitimacy. The fiery rhetoric, belligerence, and unpredictability of Kim, who took power after the death of his father in December 2011, belies an apparent hypersensitivity to criticism about his qualifications to run the country.

These responses reflect weakness, not strength. The regime has proven hypersensitive to questions about Kim's legitimacy, suggesting difficulties in the leadership transition. Four years into his rule, Kim has purged and executed around 70 of his top lieutenants, including his influential uncle Jang Song Thaek, and his defense minister Hyon Yong Chol. And these are Kim's people—not those of his father and predecessor Kim Jong Il.

The regime is tightening political control at a time when North Korean society is slowly but surely changing. Markets have been embedded in society for over two decades, but a nascent civil society may be growing around these markets as they become more central to peoples' lives. Defector testimonies indicate that people gain more of their livelihood from the markets than from government handouts, which means greater separation from the state.

Despite crackdowns by the regime, more news is finding its way into and out of North Korea. News about the outside world is slipping into the closed society through advanced technology and other smuggling methods. A hot item in North Korea today is the $50 Notel portable media player—which can play thumb drives with news about the outside world, movies, and South Korean soap operas. There are also now nearly 3 million cellphones in North Korea. Some smuggled cellphones are used not only for business and trade but also to gain outside information and communicate with relatives who have fled the North. These communication channels funnel news from the inside to the outside, allowing the world to understand more about North Korea's internal situation. The work of the U.N. Commission of Inquiry, NGOs, and several high-profile defectors have also brought much-needed global attention to issues like North Korean human rights.

The growing space between the people and the regime, the core elite and Kim Jong-un, as well as increasing external pressure are all good reasons for the North Korean leadership to be concerned. These conditions may not lead to the immediate collapse of the North Korean regime but they are certainly evidence of its growing vulnerabilities. And the last thing that North Korea wants to do is project weakness under a new leader.

Thus 2016 may witness the regime pursuing a strategy that is designed to do the opposite, that is, attempt to project an image of North Korea's military strength and Kim Jong-un's control over the elite. A new series of low-level provocations designed to showcase North Korea's military capabilities without provoking a full-scale war may be in the offing. The danger of escalation from such provocations is ever-present on the peninsula, but miscalculation by the young and unpredictable leadership is equally if not more concerning, and could determine the tenor of the crises to come in 2016.

PART VI
Africa

19. Rising Africa Faces a Critical Test

Jennifer G. Cooke

After more than a decade of strong economic growth, expanding investment flows, and narratives of a continent on the rise, sub-Saharan Africa is heading into a tough year, as some of the continent's largest economies face significant setbacks and potentially volatile political transitions. With the collapse of global oil and mineral prices, China's economic slowdown, and diminishing access to international financing, 2016 will offer an important reality check for many African governments and some hard lessons on the limits of growth without vision, diversification, and broad-based development. The coming downturn could prompt renewed impetus for critical reforms and smart public investments by some African leaders, but it could also drive greater political volatility in a number of countries whose stability is generally taken for granted in U.S. policy circles.

Responses in Nigeria, South Africa, and Angola will be particularly telling in this period, with continent-wide implications. These are the subcontinent's three largest economies and those with whom the Obama administration has sought (with decidedly mixed success) to foster strategic partnership and engage as regional interlocutors.

Angola, authoritarian but largely stable since the end of a decades-long civil war in 2002, is the most worrisome of the three. Oil production accounts for some 45 percent of the country's GDP and 70 percent of government revenues. Continued low oil prices will mean even deeper cuts to public spending as the government burns through foreign exchange reserves and faces a ballooning deficit, even as the president's family and inner circle maintain levels of conspicuous personal consumption that rival those of the world's most venal oligarchs. Spending cuts will take a toll on ordinary Angolans, who over the last two years have mounted unprecedented—albeit peaceful—public protests against the government, demanding civil liberties, basic services, and wage increases. The government has responded with disproportionate force—including against veterans protesting over pension payments—and is clearly sensitive to the possibility of expanding disorder.

Even more threatening to the regime will be the decline in resources available to fuel the president's vast patronage network that holds the increasingly restive ruling party together, including the country's politically powerful military generals. President Edoardo dos Santos, in power for 36 years, is expected to run again in the 2017 national elections, but bitter succession battles within the ruling party combined with an increasingly aggrieved and angry populace have many Angolan activists warning of major political upheaval before then.

South Africa, long considered by U.S. companies as the "investment gateway to Africa," is also headed for a turbulent year. Low commodity prices have hit the mining sector hard. Mine closures, worker layoffs, and mounting (sometimes violent) labor strikes have deepened political divisions within the ruling African National Congress (ANC) as politically powerful unions battle each other and threaten the basic political compact that has held the disparate parts of the ANC together. Cronyism and poor management in the country's state-owned enterprises have had crippling results, particularly in the power sector, which saw 100 days of rolling blackouts in the first 182 days of 2015. Unemployment officially stands at 25 percent, and compounding the many hardships faced by the country's poorest, a potentially record-breaking El Niño has already led to water shortages and cut the country's maize production—a basic food staple—by one-third in 2015. In October, university students launched nation-wide protests against tuition hikes and more broadly against the enduring disparities in access to quality education.

While the country reels from these multiple economic blows, government leadership is distracted by deepening political infighting, by mounting challenges from the populist (and largely obstructionist) Economic Freedom Fighters (EFF) and the right-leaning Democratic Alliance (DA), and by a series of major corruption scandals in which the country's top leadership is implicated. These battles will play out on a national scale in the 2016 municipal elections, and the sense of policy drift and mismanagement is unlikely to abate. The country is not likely to be fundamentally destabilized, but U.S. policymakers should not expect any constructive policy dialogue in this period, much less an enhanced South African role in continental peace and development concerns. In fact, U.S.-South Africa government relations may continue to sour, as party leaders increasingly use "anti-imperialist" rhetoric to deflect critics and forestall any real strategic introspection.

Ironically, Nigeria, which has evinced the most concern in U.S. policy circles as a country on the brink of economic and political collapse, is better positioned to weather the downturn. Peaceful elections in 2015 significantly diffused mounting national tensions, and newly elected President Muhammadu Buhari has made some promising early moves in tackling corruption, which costs the government billions of dollars annually. Oil revenues account for some 70 percent of government revenues, but just 14 percent of overall GDP. Nigeria's economy will likely be resilient, more so if the new government is able to move quickly to expand the tax base, staunch leakages, and vigorously pursue some of the reforms—in power, agriculture, infrastructure, and banking—that its predecessor set in motion. The country has made significant advances against the Boko Haram insurgency in the past year, and the U.S. security partnership, the source of considerable friction under former president Jonathan, has improved. Nigeria will not always be an easy partner but its demographics, economic dynamism, and fundamentally open society should ensure that it remains a top priority for U.S. long-term engagement in Africa.

The ill winds of economic downturn in 2016 may end up delivering some good. For new and prospective energy producers—Ghana, Tanzania, Mozambique, and Uganda, for example—the crisis could generate greater willingness to engage on issues of reform, transparency, strategic planning, and economic safeguards. For countries less reliant on primary commodities but that have nonetheless posted strong economic gains—Kenya, Côte d'Ivoire, and Ethiopia, for example—the regional downturn should give greater confidence and will offer a strong selling point to potential investors and development partners. For U.S. policy, which during President Obama's tenure has put greater emphasis on trade facilitation, technical capacity-building, and encouraging investments in critical infrastructure (notably electricity), the challenges of 2016 may expand openings for engagement, or at least identify those partners most committed to reforms.

20. Terrorism in Sub-Saharan Africa

Thomas M. Sanderson

The mass exodus of Syrian refugees gripped the world's attention in 2015. Thousands of civilians fled the civil war and navigated treacherous waters and hostile borders to reach safety in Europe. In a strategically vital region notorious for political violence, these events drew the world's attention and energy. But even as the fighting rages across Syria, Iraq, and Libya, we must look to the threat posed by escalating terrorism and violence in sub-Saharan Africa.

The 1998 bombings of U.S. embassies in Kenya and Tanzania resonate with many Americans—it was their first encounter with al-Qaeda and Osama bin Laden. As details emerged of bin Laden's earlier training facilities in Sudan, and the participation of East Africans in al-Qaeda, it was clear the region had been overlooked as a more significant threat.

The subsequent September 11, 2001, attacks focused counterterrorism efforts primarily on Afghanistan and Iraq. But signs of sub-Saharan Africa's threat to American security continued to appear. In 2008, the first American suicide bomber, Shirwa Ahmed, killed himself in Somalia at the direction of the terrorist group al-Shabaab. One year later, a young Nigerian man—recruited and trained by al-Qaeda in the Arabian Peninsula—attempted to destroy an airliner over Detroit on Christmas Day. Despite this, the region has failed to garner sufficient attention beyond efforts such as the U.S.-led Trans Sahara Counterterrorism Partnership.[1]

Today, sub-Saharan African threats are more widespread, sophisticated, and complicated to address. Three distinct, multistate areas now play host to violent extremist groups with regional ties, as well as some with connections to ISIS and al-Qaeda. These areas include the Sahel (al-Qaeda in the Islamic Maghreb, al-Mourabitun, and Ansar al-Dine); the Lake Chad Basin (Boko Haram); and the Horn of Africa/Somalia (al-Shabaab). Dozens of local armed groups operate among them.

All three areas began with groups promoting mostly locally contained, pragmatic agendas. They have now spread into more regional, ideologically oriented movements. At various points, these groups gained control of significant territory and dominated licit and illicit trade. Al-Shabaab controlled the southern half of Somalia, funding itself through taxation and the charcoal trade. AQIM and Ansar al-Dine seized northern Mali where trafficking in consumer goods, humans, drugs, and wildlife are rife. Boko Haram erupted across three northern Nigerian states, sustaining itself through kidnapping, trafficking, and a still-nebulous network of local and regional supporters.

All of these groups took advantage of ungoverned or poorly governed areas, imposing their own harsh form of control. From there, they have expanded internationally, drawing inspiration (and in some places, technical and tactical support) from ISIS and al-Qaeda. Boko Haram, for example, has greatly improved its media skills with assistance from ISIS technical experts.

These advances have not gone unnoticed, and regional forces have responded. Kenya is attempting to root out al-Shabaab militants, following attacks on the Westgate shopping mall and Garissa University. A new government in Nigeria has vowed to identify and curb regional and domestic sources of supply and funding for Boko Haram. And recently, more concerted Nigerian efforts, supported by South African contractors and neighboring forces, have pushed Boko Haram out of towns and into camps scattered across the region.

[1] For more on the TSCTP, see Lesley Anne Warner, "Nine Questions about the Trans Sahara Counterterrorism Partnership You Were Too Embarrassed to Ask," April 8, 2014, http://warontherocks.com/2014/04/nine-questions-about-the-trans-sahara-counter-terrorism-partnership-you-were-too-embarrassed-to-ask/.

In the Sahel, French and African Union forces (notably from Chad) dispersed militants who controlled the northern half of the country in 2012. But today, violence extends across much of Mali and over the border into the Ivory Coast, Burkina Faso, and Niger.

With U.S. interests threatened in the Middle East, many wonder if America can afford to mount a similar campaign in a region with fewer priorities and threats. But this concern is unfounded. The groups in question do not possess the sophistication of ISIS. But they are operating in a much more permissive environment where capacities are low and where corruption is high. The many factors leading to radicalization remain in place, so recruitment potential is elevated. The region remains susceptible to greater instability and violence.

A primary concern is that changes across the Middle East could hasten the movement of fighters to other areas with ongoing conflicts, safe havens, and like-minded groups. Libya has long meddled in sub-Saharan Africa via its long, porous southern border, through which ISIS may one day flee its redoubt in Sirte. Many foreign fighters in Syria and Iraq hail from African countries, and could well make their way to a new battlefield—fortifying existing groups. ISIS has also called on its followers to attack in place if they cannot reach their self-declared Caliphate. That sub-Saharan Africa could be the next center of gravity for jihadist violence is a real possibility.

Any such migration southward by these violent extremists would bring them to countries ill-equipped to handle them. With extremist violence already high, the arrival of battle-hardened fighters from the Middle East would devastate sub-Saharan Africa.

The United States and its partners must not wait for this to happen before shoring up regional capacities. We have to acknowledge that sub-Saharan Africa is not a tier-one priority for the United States. But on top of interests in safeguarding human rights in the region, nations such as Nigeria and Kenya serve as strategic hubs, and drive growth on the continent. America increasingly relies on them militarily, economically, and politically.

The United States should redouble its efforts to prevent sub-Saharan Africa from serving as a place for violent extremists to regroup, exchange ideas, refine technical capacities, and organize. Essential activities include greater border control; hard-nosed diplomacy to stimulate host-nation action; improved and expanded training, equipping, and coordinating of regional forces; extensive programming in countering violent extremism; enhanced intelligence sharing; and economic-development programs to provide youth with a positive future that for many seems out of reach.

PART VII
Inside the Pentagon

21. Fiscal Futures, U.S. Forces, and Strategic Choices

Mark Cancian and Todd Harrison

Defense strategy is ultimately about choices. While strategy should, in principle, drive budget decisions, strategy must also align with the resources available, or it will not be executable in practice. The U.S. military is currently experiencing a high degree of fiscal and strategic uncertainty as a result of the 2011 Budget Control Act (BCA) and subsequent political stalemate. These budget constraints were set without regard to defense strategy or the threats facing the United States and its allies. At lower budget levels the United States must make increasingly difficult choices. As an abstract proposition, choice sounds fine. As concrete policy, choices are hard. Choosing means saying that the United States will not counter certain threats as aggressively or defend certain allies as effectively.

Three Fiscal Futures

In the final week of October 2015, Congress reached a deal to raise the budget caps established by the BCA of 2011. Similar to the Ryan-Murray agreement of 2013, this deal increases the budget cap for national defense by $25 billion and boosts war funding by $8 billion in FY 2016. For FY 2017, it increases the budget cap by $15 billion and maintains war funding at the same level as FY 2016. While the deal provides two years of relative stability in the budget, it leaves the BCA budget caps unchanged for the final four years of the BCA period (FY 2018 to FY 2021). Rather than try to predict a highly uncertain future for 2018 and beyond, this paper presents three alternative fiscal futures to illustrate the decision space facing senior policymakers.

President's Budget 2012. This was the budget level Secretary Gates submitted in 2011 before the BCA and that he described at the time as an adequate level for the postwar strategy. It corresponds roughly to a level many Republican presidential candidates advocate when they propose adding forces and the level of funding recommended by the bipartisan Nation Defense Panel in 2014. The political problem is that returning to this level would require an increase in defense spending of about $1 trillion above the BCA budget caps over 10 years.

President's Budget 2016. This is the budget level the president submitted in February 2015. The administration and senior military officials describe this as the minimum level required to sustain the current strategy as described in the 2014 Quadrennial Defense Review. However, this level of funding would require an increase of more than $160 billion above the BCA budget caps over 10 years.

Revised BCA Budget Caps. The default budget levels if Congress and the president cannot forge a budget agreement after 2017 are the budget caps set in the BCA.

The Force

CSIS used its Force Cost Calculator to illustrate what forces and modernization each of the alternative budget levels could produce. The table on the following page shows some of the results when these funding levels are projected through FY 2025. (CSIS's Force Cost Calculator has 120 outputs, of which these are a sample.) This approach assumes balanced changes across the force in an attempt to remain consistent with the current strategy. Of course, risks would be different at the different budget levels. Other strategies are possible, as described later, and these would produce different sets of forces.

	PB 2012	PB 2016	Revised BCA Budget Caps
ARMY	490,000 *active-duty soliders* 34 BCTs	450,000 *active-duty soliders* 30 BCTs	420,000 *active-duty soliders* 27 BCTs
NAVY	325 Ships *(12 carriers)*	305 Ships *(11 carriers)*	270 Ships *(10 carriers)*
AIR FORCE	1,280 *fighter/attack A/C* *(446 5th generation)*	1,200 *fighter/attack A/C* *(370 5th generation)*	1,100 *fighter/attack A/C* *(350 5th generation)*
MARINE CORPS	189,000 Marines	182,000 Marines	175,000 Marines

Strategic Considerations

Historically, the United States has sized its forces for two things: wartime combat operations and day-to-day forward deployments.

Wartime combat operations entail surging large forces to a high-intensity conflict, for example in Korea. As forces shrink, response timelines extend as there are fewer forces stationed forward, mobility assets are limited, and reliance on slower deploying reservists increases. Longer timelines may be acceptable, but they mean delayed counterattacks and longer wars. In extreme cases, they can mean losing politically key terrain such as an allied capital.

Day-to-day forward deployments serve several purposes: to engage partners and allies, to deter potential conflicts, and, if a crisis arises, to respond quickly. The crisis could be relieving humanitarian disasters, supporting coalition operations against countries like Libya, or rescuing American citizens caught in civil wars.

As forces shrink, day-to-day deployments would also decline, so the United States could not respond to crises as quickly and could not engage with allies as extensively. Some strategists would accept these reductions, arguing that forces can surge from the United States when needed. But absence can both discourage allies and embolden adversaries.

The United States, of course, could give priority to one challenge over others. For example, the United States could give priority to the Pacific rebalance and take additional risk in the other theaters. In this case, it would give its NATO allies the primary responsibility for countering Russia and defending the Baltic states. Although the Europeans may have the military forces and the economic resources to do this, it is not clear that they have the political will, absorbed as they are by domestic budget tensions and an immigration crisis. The United States could also hand over more responsibility for the fight against ISIS to its Middle East allies, providing intelligence and some specialized support but scaling back existing air and ground operations, but it is not clear if these countries are willing or able to fill in for the United States. Conversely the United States could scale back its rebalance to the Pacific, taking a more balanced global approach in recognition of an uncertain future.

None of these choices is necessarily unreasonable, but all signal strategic shifts and have major effects on our allies and adversaries. With the current budget stalemate in Congress, the Obama administration will likely have to accept ad hoc solutions for its remaining time in office. The strategic choices outlined here will largely fall to the next administration. The next administration will need to conduct a strategic review to meet the new challenges facing the nation, and, just as important, it must move past today's budget posturing and strike a bipartisan deal that provides the long-term resources needed to execute the strategy.

22. The Battle Over How to Save Defense Acquisition

Andrew Hunter

As expected, 2015 proved to be a big year for defense acquisition. Yes, the Marine Corps version of the F-35 Joint Strike Fighter achieved initial operational capability, the Navy laid the keel for the its newest aircraft carrier, the USS John F. Kennedy, the Air Force awarded a contract to build the first new bomber in 30 years, and the Army awarded a contract for its next tactical vehicle, the Joint Light Tactical Vehicle (JLTV).

What made 2015 a big year for acquisition, however, was not just this new hardware but some new software—namely, the flurry of statutory changes and new provisions included in the FY16 National Defense Authorization Act (NDAA). Taken together, these legislative changes represent the largest single package of acquisition legislation since the landmark Federal Acquisition Streamlining Act of 1994.

The legislation in the FY16 NDAA provides for more involvement in acquisition by the service chiefs, more acquisition authority for service civilian executives, investments in the acquisition workforce, a slew of changes to streamline previous laws, as well as mandating the creation of alternative acquisition pathways and authorities.

At the same time that Congress was taking its hammer and wrench to the acquisition system, DoD began implementing the third iteration of its Better Buying Power Initiative, focused on sustaining U.S. technical dominance by better sharing of information between DoD and industry, encouraging use of commercial technologies, and outreach to Silicon Valley.

After a busy 2015, what does all of this activity suggest will happen in the world of acquisition in 2016?

To accurately assess the impact of acquisition changes for 2016, it is important to begin at the beginning. Is the system broken? What problems are Congress and DoD trying to solve?

Some stakeholders, notably Senate Armed Services Committee Chairman John McCain, see the acquisition system as fundamentally broken and cite as their main evidence programs like the Army's Future Combat System, the Marine Corps' Expeditionary Fighting Vehicle, and the Air Force's Expeditionary Combat Support System. These programs expended billions of dollars while ultimately providing no capability because they were terminated short of production and deployment. This perspective of the acquisition system focuses on cost growth and terminated programs as the central problem in acquisition.

Others, including many acquisition officials in DoD, see the acquisition system as fundamentally sound, albeit in need of improvement. They cite as their evidence the success of systems like the F-35 and the Aegis Combat System in international competitions as evidence that the acquisition system continues to produce superior technology at prices that, while often higher than those of other nations' systems, nonetheless are competitive in the marketplace. These officials focus on maintaining the United States' technological edge and getting more value and productivity out of the acquisition system.

While these two points of view disagree on the fundamental success or failure of the current system, and place their focus on different challenges within the acquisition system, they are not fundamentally at odds with one another when it comes to solutions. They can come together in their desire for an acquisition system that is more responsive to war-fighter needs by delivering needed capability that is timely and affordable.

The area where this outcome has been most closely realized in the last 10 years is arguably in the rapid acquisition of equipment for U.S. forces operating in Iraq and Afghanistan. While both sides of the debate see this effort as a success, the two sides draw contrasting lessons.

Critics of the system note that rapid acquisition required the creation of new organizations like the Army's Rapid Equipping Force, the Joint Improvised Explosive Device Defeat Organization, the Mine-Resistant Ambush Protected (MRAP) vehicle Task Force, and the Intelligence, Surveillance, and Reconnaissance Task Force, all of which utilized new authorities to field equipment responsive to warfighter needs. They argue that success in acquisition requires operating outside the system.

System supporters note that these new organizations often functioned as a thin overlay to traditional program and contracting offices in the acquisition system that actually acquired the new systems and did the grunt work of contracting and fielding them using existing regulations and with very little need to resort to extraordinary authorities. They argue that rapid acquisition actually happened within the current system, and that the main contributions brought by the new organizations was access to flexible funding and attention from senior decisionmakers.

While the success of rapid acquisition hasn't settled the debate about whether the acquisition system is broken or sound, it does point toward ways to improve the system going forward, namely the importance of reliable and flexible funding sources and ways to rapidly resolve bureaucratic disputes over competing priorities by obtaining timely decisions from senior leadership.

So what is the prospect for progress on these issues going into 2016? It is important to remember that although the FY16 NDAA calls for extensive changes to acquisition statutes, it is far less clear that these changes will result in meaningful operational change in the acquisition system. Will the service chiefs use their new authority to engage with the acquisition system and add financial flexibility to the process? Will the implementation of changes to milestone decision authority improve the ability to resolve bureaucratic disputes over priorities? Will new acquisition pathways and authorities be implemented in a meaningful way, and if so will they support more responsive acquisition, function only at the margins, or unintentionally short circuit and damage development?

The history of acquisition reform is littered with examples of policy changes and authorities that were either never implemented, or were implemented but had effects dramatically different from those intended.

On the whole, there is significant basis for optimism on the likelihood of progress in 2016. Both DoD and Congress currently have strong leadership in place that are unusually aware of and focused on these issues. If these leaders work together, good things will happen. Nevertheless, the passage of legislation in 2015 is much more the end of the beginning than the beginning of the end. The year 2016 could very well tell us whether the sun is rising or setting on the acquisition system.

PART VIII
Evolving Threats and Capabilities

23. Space and Security

A Conversation with Sean O'Keefe

The U.S. military's increasing reliance on space-based capabilities raises a number of issues, such as how to deter threats and increase cooperation with partners and allies in space. Todd Harrison, director of CSIS's Defense Budget Analysis and senior fellow in the International Security Program, spoke with CSIS distinguished senior adviser and former NASA administrator Sean O'Keefe on security and international cooperation in space.

What is one of the most significant challenges the U.S. military faces in the space domain today?

SEAN O'KEEFE: The most difficult challenge the Defense Department articulates regularly is assured access to space, a term that means the ability to launch satellites into orbit. Since many of these satellites are quite large due to military requirements, the Department is reliant on the heavy payload capacity of the United Launch Alliance's Delta and Atlas rockets. The Air Force has been in a defensive posture for the past couple of years trying to justify why its launch requirements need to be as unique as they are because this effectively keeps the military dependent on just one provider. There is an effort underway to allow certification for SpaceX to launch military satellites, but this is still an issue that is far from resolved.

What could the United States be doing to foster greater cooperation with its allies in military space?

O'KEEFE: Looking at the access to space challenge, there are launch capabilities resident in other nations that, while foreign-sourced, could certainly augment our own launch capabilities. It may make people uneasy to see U.S. military satellites being launched from anywhere other than U.S. soil, but this is a challenge of our own choice. We have difficulty looking at broader competitive opportunities due to parochialism and concerns about being reliant on an industrial capacity we don't have immediate control over. While there may be an opportunity to break through this logjam at some point and avail ourselves of the global market for space systems, the situation does not appear to be changing anytime soon.

How is the deterioration of relations with Russia affecting U.S. civilian and military space programs?

O'KEEFE: On the civilian side, the operations, logistics resupply, and crew exchange process for the International Space Station rests entirely now on the coordination efforts of the Russians. We do not have a capacity to launch crews to the space station any longer with the retirement of the space shuttle, and we are completely beholden to the Russians to be accommodating in that regard—but so are the other partner nations involved. It is a great testimonial to the maturity of the ISS partnerships that even given the strained relations with Russia, the consortium is strong enough to keep these sustaining activities underway. How much longer it can last is anyone's guess, but at least for now it is holding up.

On the military side, there is a mixed story emerging. The United States is concerned about its continued dependence on the Russians to provide the RD-180 engines needed for the Atlas launch vehicle. The Russians seem to view it as in their best interest to keep providing these engines either because they are looking for the hard currency or are looking to maintain the relationship or some combination of the two. But the stakes are much higher for the U.S. military because this is a dramatic exposure that compounds the access to space challenge.

What can the United States do to encourage China to be a responsible member of the space community?

O'KEEFE: We are beginning to see positive signs of progress with the Chinese regarding our long-running concerns about intellectual property piracy and export-control compliance. Assuming that progress continues and we can effectively address these concerns, this will be a propitious time to invite the Chinese into the "club" of space-exploring nations. The Chinese have already demonstrated that they have the capacity for space exploration, and they have shown a remarkable ability to accelerate their pace of development—although this has in some cases been by emulating the capabilities of others. But there is no denying the fact that they have the ambition and ability to engage in space exploration—and it is not something we can prevent anyway.

During the Cold War we established, developed, and maintained relationships with the Russians for space exploration—something that could easily be emulated with the Chinese. What I found remarkable in my tenure as NASA administrator were the testimonials of so many Russian space agency officials and cosmonauts—and NASA officials and astronauts—that despite our political differences we were able to reach amicable arrangements on objective goals for space exploration that gave the U.S.-Russian relationship meaning and purpose even at the heights of the Cold War. It led to a better understanding of each other and ultimately contributed in some small part to the detente we achieved. There is a certain thawing effect that comes when we engage in space exploration as a human activity rather than a national activity.

Do we need an international code of conduct for space? If so, how should it be negotiated and enforced?

O'KEEFE: We have more than 200 years of experience working on the Law of the Sea Treaty, but we don't have anything near that kind of history when it comes to space. Until just recently, space was the domain of really just two principal powers. But the heretic in me says that's all the more reason to try.

The challenge of creating something like this for space is that the ability for enforcement is limited—it's not easy to apprehend someone or to stop another nation from accessing space. There is also a greater risk of accidental collisions with satellites or with space debris. All of these challenges make the space domain a more difficult place to regulate. It may be more feasible to reach a workable set of protocols through a bilateral agreement first, and then use that as an approach to emulate with others.

24. Nuclear Deterrence in a Disordered World

Rebecca K. C. Hersman

Whoever takes office in January 2017 is likely to inherit a nuclear landscape of greater risk, complexity, and challenge than any time since the collapse of the former Soviet Union.

In the roiling Middle East, Iran's nuclear weapons capability may be delayed, but its malign influence continues to spread as it takes clever advantage of the surrounding chaos in Iraq, the Levant, and Yemen. Saudi Arabia, Egypt, and Israel remain concerned about Iran's nuclear ambitions, raising the stakes for proliferation and extended deterrence in the region.

In Asia, North Korea's continued expansion and diversification of its nuclear arsenal and associated delivery platforms combined with Kim Jong-un's penchant for provocation and bravado, raises the risk of nuclear coercion, and undermines confidence in current deterrence approaches. Meanwhile, nuclear competition between Pakistan and India continues to grow, spurred on by Pakistan's now-open acknowledgement of a range of "tactical" nuclear weapons as part of their "full spectrum deterrence." And China, unabashed in its desire to assert greater regional dominance, is modernizing its nuclear fleet, diversifying and hardening its nuclear arsenal, and rapidly enhancing complementary capabilities in space, cyber, and advanced missile systems.

Finally, Russia is demanding an expanded sphere of influence—rejecting further arms control efforts, embracing and modernizing its nuclear weapons program, and expanding territorial claims. Russia's highly provocative "signaling" of its nuclear capabilities to nonnuclear weapons states on its periphery coupled with proxy-warfighting in Ukraine have brought the nuclear policy and deterrence underpinnings of the NATO alliance to the fore in ways not seen since in more than 20 years.

The picture at home is daunting as well. Following a series of scandals and missteps, the U.S. nuclear enterprise again came under scathing criticism in 2014, prompting reviews that pointed to a demoralized operational climate, demotivating personnel practices, insufficient leadership and oversight, and persistent budget crises as eroding the health and sustainability of the nation's nuclear enterprise writ large.

The path to reducing and managing these risks will involve a delicate balancing of interests and players. In the Middle East, the challenge will be to suppress the nuclear appetites of state and nonstate actors as instability and conflict grow across the region and Iran's economic and conventional military powers expand. In an increasingly nuclearized Asia, the United States must reinforce confidence in extended deterrence while countering nuclear competition and any related lowering of the nuclear-use threshold. And in Europe, this balancing act requires a reinvigoration of NATO deterrence and defense posture while deescalating the nascent Russian nuclear brinkmanship currently underway. At home, Congress and the executive branch must work together to ensure a healthy and sustainable nuclear enterprise despite extraordinary budgetary pressures, a highly politicized policy climate, and an international community skeptical about U.S. motives and intentions.

That balancing act requires a coherent and compelling strategy for the role of nuclear weapons in U.S. national security that has so far proven elusive: a strategy that preserves stability without provocation, builds confidence rather than prompting fear, and preserves the highest possible threshold for nuclear use while encouraging all other nuclear weapons possessors to do likewise; a strategy that acknowledges the United States as the global champion of nuclear nonproliferation and the fundamental guarantor of security against nuclear intimidation, coercion, or use. This role requires a nuclear force and posture that is not only safe, secure, and effective but also credible, demonstrable, and sustainable. And it will require American leadership—at home, with allies, and in the face of potential adversaries—for whom the disordered world ahead may be a very scary place.

25. A Need for Global Zero

Sharon Squassoni

There is nothing like nuclear weapons to add drama to conventional crises. On the anniversary of Russia's annexation of Crimea, President Putin's claim that he considered placing Russia's nuclear weapons on alert to deter retaliatory action caused more than a few strategic analysts to sit up and take notice. In light of the ongoing modernization of Russia's nuclear forces, it's fair to ask: Are nuclear weapons back in vogue? And does this mean that "global zero" is over?[1]

For the last 10 years, the strategic nuclear policy community has had to take nuclear disarmament seriously. First came the conclusion in 2007 by the four U.S. statesmen (former secretaries of state George Shultz and Henry Kissinger, former secretary of defense Bill Perry, and former senator Sam Nunn) that the risks of nuclear weapons outweighed their benefits. Other former leaders joined the debate, publishing similar opinions around the world.

Next came President Obama's Prague speech in 2009 supporting "the peace and security of a world without nuclear weapons," followed by the 2010 Nuclear Posture Review that reduced U.S. reliance on nuclear weapons in its national security strategy.

In the meanwhile, the Global Zero movement launched its am-

[1] The phrase "global zero" here refers broadly to the various strands of the nuclear disarmament movement, including a very prominent effort within the nuclear disarmament community that is known as Global Zero, initiated in 2006 by Bruce Blair and Matt Brown. Please see www.globalzero.org for more information about their specific efforts.

bitious Action Plan (2008) advocating a mix of deep bilateral, then multilateral, cuts and de-alerting. In the last three years a fledgling, government-led Humanitarian Impact of Nuclear Weapons initiative jumped into the fray. The initiative, which the United States does not support, seeks a legal ban on nuclear weapons and now has 117 signatories. More recently, the U.S. State Department launched a project with the Nuclear Threat Initiative called the International Partnership for Nuclear Disarmament Verification.

These efforts amount to more than a fringe movement to ban the bomb. Russian recidivism may tempt some strategic analysts to fall back into Cold War habits, dismissing nuclear disarmament as an old-fashioned dream (like nuclear electricity too cheap to meter). But there are a few reasons why nuclear disarmament won't go away, and why it will be important to pay attention to the array of efforts to reduce nuclear risks:

1. *Nuclear disarmament is not just a movement but an obligation.* The 1970 Nuclear Nonproliferation Treaty has long served U.S. national security interests by limiting the number of states that acquire nuclear weapons. Under the treaty, the five nuclear weapon states (the United States, the UK, France, China, and Russia) are obliged "to pursue negotiations in good faith on effective measures relating to the cessation of the nuclear arms race at an early date, and to nuclear disarmament, and to general and complete disarmament under strict and effective international control." It is far better to direct a process to develop effective measures than only react to what could be unreasonable or impractical demands from outside.

2. *The nuclear disarmament "movement" is in the game for the long run.* The first nuclear disarmament campaigns began after World War II and they have ebbed and flowed with politics and crises. At a global stockpile of over 15,000 nuclear weapons today, we are closer to zero than we were at the height of the Cold War (70,000 nuclear weapons in 1986), but still very far away. Although some advocates of disarmament have called for "timebound" frameworks or conventions to ban nuclear weapons with a pen-stroke, few believe disarmament is quick or easy. Part of the challenge will be to accli-

matize keepers of arsenals to lower and lower numbers. This has already happened over the last 30 years in the United States and Russia, as the comfort zone for levels of deployed weapons slowly has dropped from 10,000 to 3,000 to 1,000 nuclear weapons.

3. *The long-term trend is "less is more."* Russian and U.S. nuclear forces are magnitudes larger than those of any other country (both have between 7,000 and 8,000 total deployed, nondeployed, and retired warheads). Although Russia is modernizing its forces, numbers are unlikely to go up. The end of the Obama presidency does not necessarily mean the end of nuclear weapons reductions, and a Republican president might be able to secure real reductions in treaties more easily than a Democrat. Every U.S. president since Nixon has made unilateral reductions to the nuclear weapons stockpile, with the largest of those made by Republican presidents.[2]

4. *The world has changed, but nuclear weapons haven't.* Seventy years after their invention, nuclear weapons are still regarded as indispensable and prestigious by some, and atavistic and dangerous by others. They are still the currency of power, despite the fact that influence can be wielded across borders in so many other ways today. Their imperviousness to change stands in marked contrast to, for example, information technology and nanotechnology. As the world becomes increasingly interdependent and connected, the isolation these weapons require (for safety, security, and surety reasons) will become an increasingly difficult burden.

Fundamentally, the wider support for deep nuclear cuts and for measurable progress toward disarmament is rooted in the recognition that the world has changed. No longer can we compartmentalize nuclear risks—where there are weapons, fissile material, or facilities, there will be threats and risks. When President Obama called in 2009 in Prague for durable institutions to counter this "lasting threat," he wasn't referring to the nuclear disarmament movement, but they readily responded to the call. As nuclear risks rise, their nuclear messaging may become more, rather than less, attractive.

[2] Hans Kristensen, "How Presidents Arm and Disarm," October 15, 2014, http://fas.org/blogs/security/2014/10/stockpilereductions/.

26. Missile Defense and Deterrence

Thomas Karako

In the 1980s, commentators predicted that conventional precision-strike systems would become capable of strategic effects that formerly only nuclear weapons could do. Despite efforts to curtail their proliferation, the spread of delivery system technologies has instead produced a kind of "missile renaissance."

Recent technological, commercial, and geopolitical trends have contributed to a surge in the global supply and demand for unmanned, high-precision, and high-velocity delivery systems—and the means to defend against them.

Increased interest in missile-based delivery systems spans a broad spectrum, including more advanced guided rockets, artillery, and mortars (RAM), increasingly effective air defenses, antiship missiles, new ballistic and cruise missile developments, unmanned aerial vehicles, missile-boosted hypersonic boost-glide vehicles, even antisatellite weapons.

These trends also contribute to a growing sense that defenses contribute to deterrence rather than undermine it. Whereas during the Cold War we accepted mutual vulnerability to missiles for the sake of stability, today there are simply too many missiles and too much uncertainty to forgo defenses against them. States like North Korea, for instance, may have a different disposition to both conventional escalation and even nuclear employment.

Even imperfect defenses can serve a stabilizing role by managing and mitigating that risk. Given the speed of missile raids and potential for saturation, defenses may deny an aggressor's objectives, but may also buy decision time, allow for offensive responses, or find other means of controlling escalation.

Both an outgrowth and a response to this larger missile renaissance, missile defenses now represent an established component of international security. Hit-to-kill technology has advanced considerably, with demonstrated successes across all four families of systems currently deployed by the United States today: Patriot, Aegis, Terminal High Altitude Area Defense (THAAD), and Ground-Based Midcourse Defense (GMD). Kinetic intercept will likely remain a critical part of missile defense for the foreseeable future, but nonkinetic means such as directed energy will become increasingly in demand.

The future of missile defense, however, is likely to take on a very different cast. For years the missile defense mission has been defined almost exclusively as ballistic missile defense, or BMD. The future challenge of missile defense will be characterized by the larger spectrum of integrated air and missile defense, or IAMD—a wide range of missiles and unmanned systems coming from all directions.

This will be challenging. States such as China, Russia, Pakistan, North Korea, and Iran have increased their reliance on conventional systems that are characterized by increased accuracy, mobility, speed, range, countermeasures, and penetration.

The perception of the changing relation between defenses and deterrence is not unique to the United States. From Europe to the Middle East to the Asia-Pacific, states are investing significant levels of resources to defend from missile attacks that they may not be able to deter. Japan, South Korea, India, Israel, Gulf Cooperation Council (GCC) partners—and yes, Russia and China—are all devoting significant resources to the problem of detecting, tracking, discriminating, intercepting, and even preempting missile threats.

Missile defenses are now proliferating worldwide, but integrating them with deterrence requires sustained attention. Despite President Reagan's wish, nuclear deterrence is far from becoming impotent or obsolete. Missile defense is also here to stay.

27. Disrupting the Cyber Status Quo

Denise E. Zheng

Media coverage of cyber attacks has never been higher than it is today. Government officials and business executives around the world are more aware of cyber threats than ever before and taking measures to improve security. As a result, cybersecurity is one of the fastest-growing segments of the global technology industry with approximately $1.9 billion in venture capital funding in 2014 and hundreds of new cybersecurity startups.

In the past five years, the United States alone has enacted 34 new laws and 5 executive orders to improve cybersecurity, including to strengthen standards for critical infrastructure, cyber threat information sharing, and penalties to punish and deter bad actors. U.S. defense, homeland security, and law enforcement agencies have aggressively bolstered their capacity to defend against and mitigate cyber attacks through new strategies, doctrine, and planning, and by updating technology and hiring and training thousands of new personnel.

Despite efforts to improve cybersecurity, global cyber conflict is intensifying and there is limited to no improvement in our cybersecurity posture as a nation. Companies and government agencies are engaged in an increasingly difficult struggle against persistent and agile cyber adversaries. At the nation-state level, Russia, Iran, and North Korea are using coercive cyber attacks to increase their sphere of influence, while China, Russia, and Iran have conducted reconnaissance of networks critical to the operation of the U.S. power grid and other critical infrastructure without penalty. Meanwhile, cyber crime by nonstate and substate actors has become so profitable that it has surpassed the global market for trafficking of illegal drugs.[1] There is increasing frustration over the slow pace of change, as well as concern that a truly damaging cyber attack is unavoidable if we do not change the status quo.

The slow pace of progress can be attributed to our failure to address the root causes and key enablers of cyber crime and conflict. So what are the causes and enablers? A starting point would be to look at the cybersecurity problem as three separate, but interconnected parts.

The first is the end user. These are consumers, enterprises, and government agencies that rely on commercial information technology (IT) products and services. End users are terrible at managing their own security. At the most basic level, end users do not even know how to establish strong passwords or avoid clicking on malicious links. Larger organizations struggle with basic security practices, but they also have to deal with the challenges of managing a complex IT environment, including legacy systems that are difficult if not impossible to protect.

The second part is the global black market for cyber crime and the malicious actors, tools, and services available in this underground economy. As many have pointed out, the economics of cyber crime skew in favor of the attacker. Exploits are easily acquired and can be reused on multiple targets, and the likelihood of detection and punishment is low. The underground marketplace for hacking tools and services—as well as the gains from hacking—are growing in size and complexity. The ease of monetizing hacking services and the spoils from hacking have transformed cyber crime from ad hoc activities conducted by lone individuals, to a highly organized and coordinated global network of specialized hackers and exploit developers.

1 Lillian Ablon, Martin Libicki, and Andrea Golay, "Markets for Cybercrime Tools and Stolen Data," RAND Corporation, National Security Research Division, 2014, https://www.rand.org/content/dam/rand/pubs/research_reports/RR600/RR610/RAND_RR610.pdf.

IT vendors are the third part of the problem. These companies develop, manufacture, and sell IT products, sometimes riddled with exploitable software vulnerabilities. In other business sectors, from automotive and medicine and medical devices to children's toys, there are strong precedents for product liability holding companies responsible for manufacturing and design defects and failure to warn about risks associated with using the product. In contrast, most software license agreements make companies immune to liability for damages or losses caused by software flaws. Immunity from liability in this context enables companies to get away with developing insecure products, creating fodder for the underground marketplace for malicious cyber activities, and it asymmetrically exposes enterprise and consumer end users to risk.

U.S. government policies and regulation have focused on securing the end user (consumers, enterprises, government agencies), primarily through information sharing, promoting the adoption of standards and best practices, and other incentives. While improving security at the end user is a critical piece of the problem, the approach is similar to promoting holistic medicine as a cure for communicable diseases. Improving the security of commercial IT products and disrupting the enablers of black market cyber crime, however, could have a game-changing effect on our cybersecurity posture.

Law and policymakers have shied away from tackling the root causes and key enablers of cyber crime and conflict. This is usually due to a lack of understanding of the issues—either because of their technical complexity or because of political pressure from businesses that fear regulation or privacy advocates who fear "Big Brother." In the absence of a major cyber attack on the United States, political, legal, and resource constraints on government action will likely persist. But action to address root causes and enablers of cyber crime and conflict need not contradict these political and business dynamics; in some cases, addressing them may not even require changes in policy or law. Much can be done by the handful of companies that provide the majority of products and services that comprise the Internet and computer-operating systems, through more focused nudging and guidance from government.

PART IX
Energy and Security

28. Implications of Sustained Low Oil Prices

Frank A. Verrastro

Countries and companies of all sizes continue to adjust to the new economic and market realities following the oil price collapse of 2014. And while the growth in U.S. unconventional production appears to be slowly abating, the upsurge in Organization of the Petroleum Exporting Countries (OPEC) output, robust global stock levels, and ongoing uncertainty around the strength of demand suggest that the oversupply and surpluses are likely to continue well into next year, exerting continued downward pressure on prices.

For nations that derive significant government revenue and economic support from oil export sales, the downturn has been painful (prices are some 50–60 percent lower than the summer of 2014). For consumers, the price relief has been a godsend, though to date those energy savings have yet to translate into robust spending and economic growth elsewhere. For nations that both produce and consume large volumes of oil, a significant (and sustained) price drop necessarily presents a bit of a mixed bag, carrying both positive and negative implications. And while some of these impacts are evident immediately, others take a bit longer to manifest themselves.

In the United States, the largest source of incremental global oil supply growth in the last several years, after months of lower prices and reduced rig counts, the resiliency of production growth is finally beginning to roll over and show signs of stress. After reaching some 9.6 million barrels per day (mmbd) this summer—the highest oil production level experienced in 40 years—the U.S. Energy Information Administration (EIA) now forecasts 2015 output levels at 9.2 mmbd with a further decline (to 8.8 mmbd) projected for 2016.[1]

At issue, however, is the question of how low prices can go, and more importantly, how long they are likely to remain at depressed levels. Both the level and duration of the price trough have severe implications for future investment and output volumes available over the coming years. Loss of skilled workers through cost cutting and deferral or cancellation of mega projects set the stage for future price increases as investment lapses lead to gaps in new supply additions coming to market.

Consumers have clearly benefited from lower energy prices. Average household energy expenditures are expected to fall by some 17 percent in 2015 and lower oil prices are projected to translate into $700–1,000 in energy and fuel cost savings for the average American family this year.[2] But even with gasoline at $2 per gallon, a level not seen since 2004, the economy overall has seen only modest change. Job creation in August was below the monthly average of the first seven months of the year, suggesting that slower growth in some pockets of the global economy are adversely impacting sectors in the United States and elsewhere. Oil and gas sector jobs have been slashed along with energy company budgets. And consumer spending is up only a modest 3.5 percent from a year ago when energy prices were significantly higher.

The prospects for reversal anytime soon are not bright. Absent a major supply disruption or political upheaval (not out of the question given insurgency in Yemen, distress in Nigeria and Venezuela, and continued instability in Iraq, Syria, and Libya) or a resurgent rise in

[1] U.S. Energy Information Administration, "Short-Term Energy Outlook (STEO)," September 2015, http://www.eia.gov/forecasts/steo/archives/sep15.pdf

[2] Adam Sieminski, "Effects of Low Oil Prices," U.S. Energy Information Administration, February 2015, http://www.eia.gov/pressroom/presentations/sieminski_02262015_csis.pdf.

economic growth and oil demand, the last quarter of 2015 and beginning of 2016 look equally bleak for producers. Add to that the dollar strength and the likelihood of incremental new supplies coming online from places like Iran, Iraq, and Libya as well as quick-cycle U.S. wells, and you have the makings for a persistent price slump while we work off the current surplus. In the longer run, organizations as diverse as the International Monetary Fund, EIA, and the International Energy Agency plus private banks and investment houses all point to the growth benefits derived from lower energy prices, but projections of economic improvement and demand growth vary widely, a realization always seemingly challenged by other economic "headwinds."[3]

Around the globe, the economic and social impacts of the oil price collapse are stark and uneven. Conventional onshore producers in the oil-rich Middle East, including Saudi Arabia, have some of the lowest lifting costs in the world, yet (with few notable exceptions) budgets are straining as export revenues are curtailed—even if volumes are up. For countries like Iran and Russia, hampered by the combination of sanctions and low oil and gas prices, economic strife is palpable and unrelenting—and may encourage regional and geopolitical or financial alliances that were previously unthinkable.[4] For new producers in East Africa or those already economically or politically challenged (such as Venezuela, Algeria, Libya, Nigeria, Brazil, and Iraq) or in the midst of undertaking reforms (Mexico), lower revenues and less attractive investment prospects are far from good news.

From an environmental and energy security perspective, the impacts of sustained lower oil prices are also necessarily a bit more nuanced. Depending on demand elasticities, lower oil prices should, in theory, stimulate additional oil demand, while at the same time reducing the economic attractiveness of higher-priced but less-polluting en-

[3] International Monetary Fund, "Global Implications of Lower Oil Prices," July 14, 2015, http://www.imf.org/external/pubs/ft/survey/so/2015/INT071415A.htm; International Energy Agency, "Oil Market Report," https://www.iea.org/oilmarketreport/omrpublic/; U.S. Energy Information Administration, "Short-Term Energy Outlook (STEO)."
[4] Frank Verrastro, Larry Goldstein, and Guy Caruso, "Oil Markets: 'Trouble Ahead, Trouble Behind,'" CSIS, October 10, 2014, http://csis.org/publication/oil-markets-trouble-ahead-trouble-behind.

ergy forms, at least in the transport sector—not a good outcome from an environmental perspective. Additionally, lower gasoline pump prices tend to encourage more driving, the purchases of large and less fuel-efficient cars and trucks, while tamping down the demand for more expensive hybrids, gas-powered, or electric vehicles. And while public policy choices such as mandates, tax incentives, and HOV lane accessibility can be used to partially offset this "economic advantage," the opportunity to displace or replace liquid petroleum fuels in transportation is likely to be delayed by lower oil prices.

Sustained low oil prices discourage higher cost development, regardless of source, potentially subordinating security and diversity of supply considerations to one of comparative price savings. At low oil prices, the economics of more expensive liquefied natural gas (LNG) projects also come into question. Security comes in many forms, not the least of which includes having a diverse and robust global market, strategic stocks to draw prompt barrels from in times of significant shortfalls and policies that, at once, support balancing prudent and timely development of indigenous (fossil and renewable) energy resources with environmental stewardship, economic improvement, strong trade ties, and a future-oriented outlook as the energy landscape continues to change.

Nations with diversified and strong economies can benefit from price stability, recognizing that the period of 2010–13 may have been the near-term outlier in oil price terms. Those countries highly dependent on oil-export revenues, however, remain seriously challenged. Some, with strong balance sheets and robust treasuries, will survive the price downturn. Others, with fewer options and less flexibility, may not. Widespread instability and failed states are not desirable outcomes for anyone.

As we move toward the end of the year, financial and tax considerations related to inventory draws will undoubtedly influence supply decisions, even while potentially adding to the existing over supply. Oil and gas exploration are by nature capital intensive and often require years of upfront spending in terms of lease acquisition, explorations, appraisal, and development before commercial volumes are produced. Geopolitical disruptions remain a constant threat. The prospects for robust and widespread global recovery remain elusive.

The rise in unconventional oil and gas has expanded the opportunity pool of future supply, added more nations to the mix of prospective producers and already altered global energy flows. But we are still in the very early stages of development and multiple outcomes—not all desirable—have yet to be identified. Supply-demand relationships between nations will inevitably shift, intraregional trade may expand at the expense of longer-haul trade, and geopolitical alliances may be altered as a consequence.

The energy landscape remains in the midst of dynamic change. It will impact and be impacted by a number of resource, economic, governance, trade, foreign policy, security, and environmental policies and events. The dramatic growth in unconventional oil will likely extend the life of fossil fuels, and lower prices (for a time) should benefit consumers everywhere. But as with all depletable resources, underinvestment now is likely to bring unpleasant consequences in the not-too-distant future.

29. Implications of a Low-Carbon Future

Sarah O. Ladislaw

The world relies heavily on fossil fuels to meet its energy needs, and the development and trade of those fuels has influenced relationships among countries throughout modern history. Most reasonable projections of the next several decades anticipate that the role of coal, oil, and gas will be maintained but lose market share to lower-carbon energy sources like wind, solar, nuclear, and greater efficiency.

Despite the continued role for fossil fuels, the push for greater reliance on lower-carbon energy sources has made progress since it began in earnest several decades ago. Nearly $318 billion was invested in new clean energy sources around the world last year, up from $60 billion in 2004. Nearly half of this investment took place in large developing economies, particularly China but also Brazil, India, and South Africa.

The policies that promote low carbon energy are spreading as well. According to the United Nations, 39 percent of countries accounting for 73 percent of the world's population and 67 percent of greenhouse gas emissions are covered by some sort of climate law or strategy, many of which include support for low-carbon energy. While trade in low-carbon energy sources is still far behind the volume or value of traded fossil energy, investment in nonfossil power generation capacity surpassed that of new fossil-based electric power in 2014, and the supply chains involved in low-carbon energy technology development are global in nature.

Even though the world remains far away from the stated international targets of deep de-carbonization and atmospheric stabilization, the push to create low-carbon economies—societies that function and flourish using low-carbon energy sources—is slowly reshaping the geopolitics of energy in ways reflected outside trade and investment flows.

Pushing against Barriers between Developed and Developing Economies

Take one look at the UN Framework Convention on Climate Change (UNFCCC), the main body for climate change negotiations, and it is clear the world is divided into multiple and overlapping blocks of countries with shared and divergent agendas. What was once an organization divided into rich and poor country blocks is now much more complex.

While the developed and developing country divide still prevails, countries are united by a wide array of shared interests such as carbon market mechanisms, fossil-fuel subsidy reform, climate change loss and damage claims, technology transfer agreements, climate finance arrangements, and many more issues. The UNFCCC is indeed saddled with the burden of including every country on Earth, which makes progress difficult to achieve, but it also fosters new alliances that reflect the viewpoints on every side of climate debate and bolster cooperation among previously disconnected groupings of countries.

Linking Subnational and Supranational Elements

Low-carbon energy deployment is facilitated by a combination of policies, investments, and technological advancements. Traditionally those enabling environments have been the purview of national-level governments. In recent years, however, the drive for more rapid diffusion of low-carbon energy sources is driven by a mass diffusion of efforts from the international and national governance structures to subnational and nongovernmental actors.

Today, pressure to act on climate change is not entirely or even mostly an effort led by national governments. States, provinces, local communities and representatives from different sectors of the economy have banded together to reduce emissions and adapt to a changing climate.

At the supranational level one need not look farther than Pope Francis's encyclical and the statements made by other religious leaders to see how the calls for low-carbon energy development are intended to transcend national and even religious boundaries.

These sub and supranational aspects of the push for low-carbon energy and action on climate change give a multidimensional nature to the climate change issue much like other transnational issues that national governments are working to address.

Factoring into Global Institutions and Alliances

In under a decade climate change has come to be incorporated into nearly every major international energy, environmental, development, and economic institution. The G-20 has provisions on fossil fuel subsidy reform, energy market transparency and climate finance. The World Bank now takes carbon emissions into consideration when funding energy and infrastructure projects. Recent high-level, bilateral and multilateral gatherings both including and not including the United States have featured cooperation on climate change and low-carbon energy as major points of agreement and future cooperation.

The strategic objectives of these organizations and alliances are subordinate to domestic political and economic priorities, but in many cases low carbon energy has become a priority in those domestic contexts as well. The impetus for low-carbon energy promotion varies within each of these countries and institutions. For many countries the low-carbon nature of energy is second to the local pollution abatement benefits. For others, low-carbon energy represents an area of economic and technological competition. No matter the driver, low-carbon energy and climate change issues have taken on a new level of inclusion and importance in global institutions and multilateral initiatives.

The Bumpy Road Ahead

Folks who are sympathetic to the climate cause may be inclined to believe that low-carbon energy alleviates many of the world's more problematic geopolitical dynamics—like the perennial fight about natural gas between Russia and Ukraine, the need for the United States to be involved in regional conflicts in the Middle East, and tension between the United States and a rising China.

Low-carbon energy can assist by providing greater supply diversity and identifying areas of common ground, but it does not directly resolve any one of those issues. Moreover, the policies used to foster low-carbon energy sources may create some new geopolitical tensions of their own. The starkest example is the prospect for border tariff adjustments that could eventually be imposed to level the playing field between countries with and countries without effective carbon regulation.

The push toward low-carbon energy is likely to intensify as the climate community seeks greater ambition of effort and deeper mitigation commitments over the next 10 years. This will continue to reshape investment and energy trade flows within the context of other global energy and economic trends. The movement to foster these changes will also influence geopolitical alignments in subtle but important ways.

30. Efficacy of Sanctions Against Energy-Producing Countries

Edward C. Chow

Economic sanctions have become the tool of choice for American foreign policy. This is particularly true after recent painful experience with military interventions in Afghanistan and Iraq and because of the perceived success of past economic sanctions.

At a time of plentiful oil and gas supply and cyclical downturn in energy pricing, this especially applies to offending oil-producing countries, which became more vulnerable to sanctions, with seemingly little consequence to global energy markets. Sanctions against Iran over nuclear proliferation and against Russia for its aggression against Ukraine are the two most prominent current examples.

Iran was always dependent on oil revenue, which contributed more than 60 percent of government revenue and 80 percent of export earnings. Mismanagement of its economy made Iran more vulnerable to an oil embargo by the European Union and the United States, which also forced other buyers of Iranian oil to reduce their imports. As a result, Iranian oil exports were reduced by 1 million barrels per day (mmbd) with severe negative impact on the Iranian economy.

Assuming that Iran complies with the terms of the nuclear deal it reached with the five permanent members of the United Nations Security Council and the European Union, it will be allowed to resume and increase oil exports in 2016, first from tanker storage of unsold oil and subsequently from increased production. Although Iran's official production target in 2016 is to reach pre-sanctions level above 4 mmbd, it will likely take a couple of years and investment to rejuvenate declining oilfields before this target can be met. Nevertheless, even a modest but steady increase in Iranian oil exports would prolong the current slump in oil prices while extending the desire of other major oil producing countries to protect their market share.

Longer term, Iran has more ambitious plans to increase its oil production and to exploit its enormous natural gas potential to become a net gas exporter. It has begun preliminary talks with international oil companies and shown a willingness to modify contract terms in order to attract massive investments. Previous Iranian governments chased away foreign oil and gas investors, including those from friendly countries, through harsh commercial terms and difficult operating conditions, even before international sanctions came into force. This made multilateral sanctions easier to apply when they came—an object lesson perhaps for the future. However, it will take at least five years before major contracts can be negotiated and for new investment to bear fruit before further increases in Iranian oil and gas production can have any impact on the global energy market.

Under Vladimir Putin's rule, Russia has become a petro-state in ways the Soviet Union never was. Oil and gas represent 50 percent of central government revenue and 70 percent of export earnings. An import-dependent Russian economy requires oil and gas income to prosper. The ruble has lost half of its value since the oil price slump and more severe Western economic sanctions were implemented in July 2014. An already-stagnant economy has fallen into deep recession and is unlikely to recover until 2017 unless oil prices spike and until major structural economic reforms are enacted, neither of which is likely to happen.

The current Western economic sanctions were never designed to impact short to medium Russian oil and gas production. They were designed to affect longer-term prospects for production from frontier areas such as the Arctic offshore, unconventional oil (also known as shale oil or tight oil), and sales of high technology for such projects. Indeed Russian oil production remains at a post–Soviet peak and gas production is constrained more by weak demand domestically and in export markets. The ruble collapse lowered costs of Russian oil producers while their export revenue is still denominated in dollars. Russia's central government, which took the lion's share of oil revenue above $40 per barrel through the taxation system, suffered the brunt of the oil price decline, along with the inefficient general economy that the government subsidized. Western financial sanctions have a greater impact on Russian oil and gas companies, especially national champions Gazprom and Rosneft, by limiting their access to external markets to refinance their debt and to finance new investments.

As such, Western sanctions have done exactly what they were designed to do: impacting the Russian economy without negatively affecting oil and gas flows. Whether it will modify Russian behavior in Ukraine remains to be seen. It may take more time than we wish, which challenges the preservation of Western unity. Meanwhile, Russia may become more desperate in Ukraine and elsewhere to test that unity.

History should have taught us that economic sanctions alone are an imperfect tool. Sanctions against Saddam Hussein's Iraq lasted for more than a dozen years and did not change his policies very much until the United States invaded Iraq and toppled his regime. Larger countries like Russia and Iran have more policy options to defend their interests by dividing the international alliance against them without which unilateral U.S. sanctions would be ineffective. For example, Russia supplies one-third of Europe's oil and gas demand, and European economies are more interlinked with Russia than the American economy. Iran is a major oil supplier to countries such as Turkey, India, China, Japan, and South Korea, which remain interested to do business with Iran. Both Russia and Iran can accuse Washington of forfeiting the interest of our closest allies and trading partners since America is less dependent on imported energy than they are.

Major energy-producing countries can form temporary alliances of convenience to evade sanctions, such as what Russia is currently attempting to do with China. Temporary actions can develop into more permanent conditions with significant geopolitical consequences. As a permanent member of the Security Council, Russia in particular can block UN action in other areas and use its political and military influence in situations such as the civil war in Syria and the fight against the Islamic State. Iran is a regional power in the energy-critical Persian Gulf and an increasingly fragmented Middle East, a position it can use for good or ill.

Much of the effectiveness of U.S. economic sanctions is derived from the dominance of American financial institutions and use of the dollar in international commerce, and the threat of secondary sanctions against violators of multilateral sanctions. This puts a premium on arriving at internationally agreed multilateral sanctions, which is more difficult against major energy-producing countries and involves a process that often leads to the lowest common denominator to the annoyance of U.S. policymakers. It also increases the incentive for major energy-producing countries under the threat of sanctions to create alternative international payment, insurance, and other financial systems that avoid Western institutions in cooperation with major energy-importing countries, such as China and India, which wish to chart their own independent course of foreign policy.

The fact that economic sanctions take a long time to become effective and are slow in achieving their policy objective of changing the behavior of offending countries often frustrates U.S. policymakers. The temptation then is for Washington to ratchet up sanctions unilaterally, if necessary. In the case of sanctions against major energy-producing countries, this can lead to the fracturing of the coalition enforcing sanctions and to a more determined adversary seeking to evade sanctions and threaten retaliation elsewhere.

Economic sanctions are not the silver bullet when used against major countries, especially those that produce a critical, fungible, and widely traded commodity. They should be used judiciously, along with other statecraft such as diplomacy and the threat of force. The objective should be to bring the offending country to the negotiation table for a more permanent solution. A case in point is the nuclear negotiations with Iran and the hoped-for resolution in 2016. An even more challenging case will be Russia and settlement of the crisis in Ukraine, triggered by its aggressive actions, which will likely be with us beyond 2016. These will not be the last time economic sanctions will be waged against oil-producing countries. No doubt their lessons will continue to be learned and relearned by all.

PART X

Human Rights, Human Security, and Public Diplomacy

31. Responding to the Closing of Democratic Space

Shannon N. Green

After nearly four decades of unrivaled expansion, democracies worldwide appear to be back on their heels. Authoritarian regimes, semi-authoritarian regimes, and new and fragile democracies are increasingly constricting civil and political rights, intensifying pressure on civil society and human-rights defenders, cracking down on independent media, appropriating the Internet and social media to propagate alternative truths and monitor critics, and broadening the powers and reach of internal security services, often under the guise of countering terrorism. According to Freedom House, in 2014, for the ninth year in a row, nearly twice as many countries experienced declines to civil liberties and political rights as registered gains.[1]

Perhaps more ominously, the repressive tactics and ambitions of many states extend beyond the domestic sphere. Authoritarian governments are increasingly sharing "worst practices." For example, prohibitions on foreign funding for certain political or human rights activities that originated in Russia quickly spread to Ethiopia, India, Venezuela, and Zimbabwe.[2] And other countries, such as Ecuador, Hungary, Iran, Rwanda, Turkey, and Uganda, appear to be looking to

---

[1] Freedom House, *Freedom in the World 2015* (Washington, DC: Freedom House, 2015), 1–29, https://freedomhouse.org/report/freedom-world/freedom-world-2015.

[2] Thomas Carothers and Saskia Brechenmacher, "Closing Space: Democracy and Human Rights Support under Fire," Carnegie Endowment for International Peace, 2014, 1–90.

China for inspiration and reassurance that it is possible to usher in an era of increased economic prosperity and modernity, while maintaining political power and controls.

Finally, authoritarian governments are using their participation in multilateral institutions, such as the United Nations Human Rights Council, to erode international norms and standards on democracy and human rights and shield themselves from criticism for their antidemocratic behaviors. As a result, democracy—and the system of democratic values and norms that has been built up over the past few decades—is increasingly under assault around the world.

The question facing us now is what kind of century we have lying ahead: one characterized by a brief period of democratic stagnation or backsliding or one in which we will see a prolonged democratic recession? Part of the answer lies in how democracies themselves respond. As authoritarian models gain traction globally, the United States and its democratic allies must mount a concerted effort to reassert democratic values and reestablish democracy's prestige. This starts with making democracy deliver.

Democracy's appeal has been weakened by chronic political and economic crises in longstanding democracies, and the seeming inability of those in power to decisively confront these challenges. The global financial crisis that began in 2007—and still reverberates in sluggish wage growth in the United States, high unemployment rates in much of Europe, and the near-collapse of the Eurozone over Greece's debt—undermined the belief that democracies are uniquely positioned to deliver prosperity. Likewise, the refugee and migrant crisis in Europe, and the at-times chaotic and brutal response to it, have called into question the ability of advanced democracies to collectively respond to complex emergencies and abide by their international commitments.

Finally, the annual threat of a government shutdown in the United States and the perpetual inability of the Congress to pass a budget have created doubts about whether democracies are capable of performing even the most basic governance functions. The Obama administration recognized the impact of gridlock on America's standing, concluding in the 2015 National Security Strategy that political dysfunction "undermines national unity, stifles bipartisan cooperation, and ultimately erodes the perception and strength of our leadership abroad."[3]

Despite these warning signs, democracy retains significant strengths and is still the preferred system of government in most countries, according to regular global surveys. And autocracies are not immune from political dysfunction or economic misfortunes, as the recent slowdown in China demonstrates. Reclaiming democracy's momentum will require the United States and other established democracies to get their own houses in order and recommit to partnership and joint action.

The Community of Democracies (CD) was established in 2000 for just this purpose—as a unique platform for democratic countries to come together to support the consolidation of democratic values and practice around the world. Since its inception, the CD has spawned several important working groups and initiatives, including efforts to engage with and defend civil society against increased governmental restrictions.

Yet, the CD has failed to become a preeminent, high-level platform for meaningful collective action by democracies to support and defend democracy. With the United States in the presidency, it is an opportune time to upgrade the CD and make it a venue for genuine policy coordination and action, as well as a counterweight to institutions like the Shanghai Cooperation Organization, which are being used to advance nondemocratic agendas.

The present setbacks for democracy also offer an opportunity to radically rethink dominant approaches to democracy promotion and support for civil society. It is widely acknowledged that a strong, vibrant civil society is essential for innovation and progress and for holding governments accountable for delivering on democracy's promise. Civil society's role is so important that President Obama made supporting and defending civil society a priority for U.S. agencies engaged abroad.

[3] Barack Obama, *National Security Strategy* (Washington, DC: The White House, February 2015), 1–29, https://www.whitehouse.gov/sites/default/files/docs/2015_na-tional_security_strategy_2.pdf.

But herein lies the dilemma. What if, despite our best intentions, support to civil society is actually contributing to closing space? Increasingly, research and experience point to a correlation between a heavy reliance on external sources of funding and weak links between civil society organizations and local populations—leaving these organizations vulnerable to accusations that they are serving a foreign agenda and alienated from the communities they are meant to serve.[4] The dependence on short-term, donor-driven, project-based funding also draws organizations away from their core missions and the needs of their communities in pursuit of scarce resources. In a recent essay, Ford Foundation President Darren Walker labeled this system a "tyranny of donors—that distorts and inhibits, rather than unleashes, the potential of civil society."[5]

The good news is that there are steps that donors can take to reverse this tide, beginning with making long-term, strategic investments in proven civil society organizations. Some aid organizations are already changing the way they do business, emphasizing the need for civil society to cultivate grassroots constituencies, encouraging partners to pursue local sources of funding, and diversifying their grantees beyond the usual, capital-based organizations.[6]

This approach is not without its risks. Donors will have to accept that progress cannot always be measured in discrete deliverables or with quantitative indicators, going against the current fixation with using scientific approaches and data to assess impact. Change will also require shifting the emphasis from the donor's priorities to investing in the core mission of civil society partners. As an activist recently told me, "Don't come here to ask me to execute your strategy, but to help me execute my strategy." These ideas, while heretical to some and difficult to put into practice, will help restore account-

[4] Sarah E. Mendelson, *Why Governments Target Civil Society and What Can Be Done in Response: A New Agenda* (Washington, DC: CSIS, April 2015), 1–11, http://csis.org/files/publication/150422_Mendelson_GovTargetCivilSociety_Web.pdf.

[5] Darren Walker, "How Can We Help You?" State of Civil Society Report, Ford Foundation, 2015, 1–7, http://civicus.org/images/SOCS2015_ESSAY27_HowCanWeHelp.pdf.

[6] Thomas Carothers, "Democracy Aid at 25: Time to Choose," *Journal of Democracy* 26, no. 1 (January 2015): 59–73.

ability between civil society organizations and the communities they serve—putting civil society once again at the heart of safeguarding democracy.

Even if we do employ more effective strategies for empowering civil society and staunching the closing of civic space on a case-by-case basis, it remains to be seen whether the United States and its democratic allies are willing to contest the ground in this new war of ideas. There is a strong case for elevating the focus on democracy and human-rights promotion and leading with our values. Democratic countries are less prone to give rise to terrorists, proliferate weapons of mass destruction, or engage in aggressive behavior. The United States also has a moral responsibility to stand with those struggling for greater freedoms and human rights.

Perhaps most importantly, we cannot hope to defeat Russian propaganda or the Islamic State's social media onslaught without a more powerful, values-based narrative of our own. Despite these factors, U.S. policy has been slow to recognize and respond to the growing threat posed by resurgent authoritarians. In part to distance itself from the Bush administration's Freedom Agenda and its related misadventures in Iraq, the Obama administration has tended to take a pragmatic, transactional approach to authoritarian regimes and invest in multilateral initiatives, like the Open Government Partnership, that provide incentives for governments to improve transparency, accountability, and relations with civil society.

The next president will have a critical choice to make as he or she confronts an increasingly hostile world for democratic values and practices: will he or she embrace democracy and human rights promotion as a central aim of U.S. foreign policy or continue to let democracy's standing wither?

32. Soft Power and Security

Daniel F. Runde

International development assistance has been a critical tool for expanding political freedom, economic progress, and global security since the Marshall Plan following World War II. The security challenges facing the United States are broad and varied, and an effective administration will use the full array of tools at its disposal. In some cases, a military response to a security challenge is not the best option available. Ideally, we defuse threats before they manifest by expanding and strengthening the rules-based order that the United States and its allies constructed over the last 70 years. One of the most important questions facing the next American president will be: How do we apply development assistance and other forms of soft power to increase our security?

If American taxpayers are going to continue to support the U.S. foreign assistance budget, which at roughly $30 billion annually makes us the most generous nation on Earth, they need to know that this money is well spent and that it makes them more secure. This means addressing threats to core U.S. interests, and doing so in an effective and accountable manner. International assistance is a reflection of national generosity, but at a strategic level it aims to help countries develop economically and socially so that they can become net contributors to the rules-based world order.

A few ongoing challenges that the United States should address (at least in part) through strategic foreign assistance are: the threat of global pandemics like the Ebola outbreak in the fall of 2014; security and humanitarian issues arising from immigration crises at U.S. and European borders; instability and security threats arising from radical extremism; and confronting great-power threats to the rules-based world order. All of these challenges demand cooperative solutions that leverage military, diplomatic, and economic assets from countries interested in upholding global security and prosperity.

There is no question that development spending can be a safeguard for stability and security when deployed effectively. It must be stated, however, that major global progress on a number of fronts over recent decades has changed the way foreign assistance should be utilized. The world is freer, more prosperous, and has greater capacity than at any time in human history. The largest drivers of international development are private-sector activity and good governance (with a bias toward democratic governance). International assistance can catalyze these forces, but donors no longer hold the largest wallet in the room. In a world where total foreign direct investment and tax dollars collected in developing countries are orders of magnitude larger than official development assistance (ODA), donors need to recognize their role as facilitators, providers of expertise, and catalytic investors.

Despite these changes, international assistance still has an important role to play, and has underpinned global economic and social development in ways that support U.S. security and prosperity. Historically, U.S. foreign assistance has been strikingly effective. Nineteen of 20 top U.S. trading partners are former assistance recipients, including key partners like Germany, Japan, South Korea, and Taiwan. These successes demonstrate the potential of foreign assistance to transform the world for the better. There are, however, a series of critical questions the United States should be asking itself to ensure that our assistance dollars are leveraged in the most effective way possible.

Are our assistance agencies organized appropriately? As it stands, the United States has over 20 agencies that help deliver U.S. foreign assistance. This has led to fractured goals and policy, and limits our ability to deliver impact. Presidents Johnson and Nixon had one single aid agency that coordinated all assistance activity. In an era where there are coordinators and czars for seemingly every government activity, there is an argument to be made for a consolidated aid apparatus.

Does our assistance spending aim to leverage and catalyze larger forces? Private-sector activity, investment, and domestic resources collected in developing countries themselves will provide the bulk of development finance over the coming decades. We should be designing our aid programs to enable private-sector growth and support effective and transparent governance.

Do our aid agencies have the right human resources and human-resource strategies? U.S. foreign assistance capability would benefit greatly from a special expeditionary force that is equipped and trained to operate in less than stable environments. This would include conflict zones as well as failed and failing states. We should also consider much longer commitments for personnel operating in conflict countries contemplating tours of duty as long as eight years in one country. Providing the necessary training and incentive structure for this force may require specialized college scholarship programs.

Do current regulations maximize the potential impact of international assistance spending? Current constraints on resources, including inflexible uses for monies, arduous inspectors general oversight, an outdated Foreign Assistance Act, and a constraining rule book for procurement, limit our ability to deliver effective assistance. Longer project timelines that extend beyond 3 to 5 years should be replaced with projects with 7- to 15-year time horizons. This is especially true in the conflict zones and failing states that have the most pressing need for assistance.

Today the world faces a complex and growing list of shared challenges. As has been the case since World War II, the United States and our allies have the task of supporting a rules-based global order. Following China's creation of the Asian Infrastructure Investment Bank (AIIB), we face true geostrategic competition in the soft-power arena. We need to be cognizant that we must offer the types of assistance that developing countries themselves want, or they now have the option of taking their business to China. This pressure on us and our allies could be positive if it forces a modernization and rethink of our approach to international assistance.

The globalization of trade, investment, and commerce has left us with a world that is more integrated than ever, but has also led to the rise of transnational threats that undermine security and economic prosperity. Now more than ever, the task of upholding global security and facilitating economic and social development requires the cooperation of likeminded nations capable of harnessing military, diplomatic, and economic tools in coordination to achieve positive outcomes. Foreign assistance, when deployed effectively, is a big part of this picture.

33. After the Ebola Catastrophe

J. Stephen Morrison

As 2015 unfolded, the worst of the Ebola catastrophe had ended, leaving in its wake a terrible trail. Ebola has, as of November 2015, killed more than 11,000 (including over 500 health workers) and infected more than 30,000. Thousands of survivors today struggle with heavily impaired personal health, amidst heavily damaged national health systems.

The global response, tragically late by several months and organized in extreme haste in late 2014, was, in effect, a $5 billion scramble. It unfolded amid widespread panic, fear, and chaos. Today, the outbreak is under control, though it persists at very low levels and the region may not be effectively cleared of the virus. In the course of this suffering and its aftermath, accountability has been elusive. It is difficult to name a single official—international, national or otherwise—who was fired.

There were many moments of exceptional courage, sacrifice, and impromptu brilliance. Doctors Without Borders (MSF) were true heroes, as were countless less well-known Liberian, Sierra Leonean, and Guinean individuals, civil organizations, and government health officers. Cooperation accelerated across governments, regulatory bodies, industry, and the World Health Organization to advance the testing of vaccines and antivirals. U.S. leadership, though late, was pivotal to bringing the outbreak under control: the U.S. Agency for International Development (USAID) and the Centers for Disease

Control and Prevention (CDC) each distinguished themselves, field-
ed hundreds of American staff on the ground, and accounted for no
less than half of the international response. The 2,800 U.S. troops
deployed to Liberia were strategically important in breaking panic
and opening logistical operations. Congress in December 2014 ap-
proved $5.4 billion in emergency Ebola funding, of which $3.7 billion was to complete the job of control in West Africa, continue to
advance the development of new scientific and medical tools, and
build basic health security capacities.

Soul Searching Begins

Ebola also triggered considerable introspection in 2015 by no fewer than four international panels.[1] Many feel, it seems, that this historical—and preventable—failure warrants in-depth introspection
and a concrete plan of action for the future.

I served on the Independent Panel on the Global Response to Ebola, organized by the Harvard Global Health Institute and the London
School of Hygiene and Tropical Medicine, which released its full report in November. The panel struggled with answering two fundamental questions. How are we to make sense of—and account for—
the wide-ranging, egregious failures to prepare, detect, and respond?
And most important and arguably most urgent, what are the next
steps to restore confidence and trust that when the next outbreak
occurs, the world is reliably better prepared? That means ensuring
that there will be robust high-level political leadership. It means taking steps to build core capacities in vulnerable countries. It rests on
external assistance being mobilized quickly and effectively, and ensuring that medical tools, protections of workers, and knowledge of
best practices are available. And it rests on strengthening the inter-

[1] These include the Ebola Interim Assessment Panel, chaired by Dame Barbara Stock-
ing, which issued its final report in July 2015; the Independent Panel on the Global
Response to Ebola, organized by the Harvard Global Health Institute and the London
School of Hygiene and Tropical Medicine; the Commission on a Global Health Risk
Framework for the Future, organized by the Institute of Medicine; and the UN Secre-
tary General's High-Level Panel on Global Response to Health Crises.

national organizations and other institutions charged with leading a coherent response so that they are competent, speedy, and accountable, and that they operate according to an agreed set of priorities and responsibilities.

So What Is to Be Done?

There are many answers detailed in the panel's 10 primary recommendations. Two considerations are of penultimate importance.

First, now is the time to act—at a high level—if the opportunity to effect real change in how the world prepares for infectious outbreaks is not to slip away. The risk is we return to business as usual, with modest reforms on the margins, and continued high vulnerability.

The perceived threat of Ebola has declined precipitously, as other crises muscle their way onto center stage. The most prominent, of course, is the worsening global disorder, centered in the Middle East and North Africa, that is contributing to a colossal human crisis (millions of Syrian refugees in neighboring states, 500,000 refugees entering Europe in 2015) that now dominates airwaves and high-level political debate, alongside consideration of Russia's expanded military role in the widening Syrian war.

The much weakened WHO Director General Margaret Chan are simply in no position to carry forward an agenda of deep structural change in how the world prepares for infectious outbreaks: that can only come from a committed and determined nucleus of North and South heads of state and other high-level leaders.

How might that nucleus form? That is far from certain but still possible. It may emerge from German president Merkel, who in her role as chair of the 2015 G-7 rallied other G-7 members around a shared commitment to follow through with major reforms in the global approach to disasters like Ebola, as the picture settles and the work of investigative panels is completed. It is hoped that Merkel will receive aid from Japanese prime minister Abe, who will chair the G-7 in 2016 and has indicated his desire to carry forward the commitments made by G-7 members in Berlin. And UN secretary general Ban Ki-moon and members of the UN Security Council will play potentially pivotal roles, along with leaders of Liberia, Sierra Leone, and Guinea, as well as the Africa Union. All four investigative panels will have completed their work by year's end, will overlap to a considerable degree, and can help spur high-level debate in 2016. Any further dangerous outbreaks, such as MERS (Middle East Respiratory Syndrome) or pandemic flu, will concentrate attention but can hardly be predicted.

Second, fixing WHO needs to be the top priority. That is the single most conspicuous requisite for restoring the trust and confidence of the world's leaders that there will not be a repeat of the Ebola catastrophe when the next outbreak occurs. Half measures will not suffice. If WHO is not fixed, the world's powers will revert tacitly to plan B: assume the worst on the part of WHO, and assume the United States, other major powers, the UN Security Council, and UN agencies will again scramble, in an ad hoc and chaotic fashion, to piece together a response.

The WHO Executive Board commissioned a panel, chaired by Dame Barbara Stocking, which completed its work in July and made several recommendations: the establishment of a Center for Emergency Preparedness and Response; modest budget increases; and a $100 million pandemic response fund. A committee will consider incentives for early notification of emergency outbreaks and steps to deter unwarranted disruptions of trade and travel.

These changes, while worthwhile, simply do not go far enough. The newly formed WHO Emergency Center needs to be much more than a simple merger of outbreak response and humanitarian emergency capacities. It needs to be muscular and autonomous: to have an independent director and board, be able to fulfill a full range of critical functions. The latter include support to governments in building core capacities; rapid early response to outbreaks; technical norms and guidance; and convening parties to agree upon a strategy that sets clear goals and effectively mobilizes money and political will.

The decision power within WHO for declaring an emergency needs to be moved from the WHO director general to a Standing Emergency Committee that is far more technically competent, transparent, and politically protected.

WHO needs to step into the lead in developing a framework of rules for the sharing of data, specimens, and benefits during outbreak emergencies.

Deep internal reforms of WHO, long overdue, are essential if member countries are to be persuaded to invest in it seriously over the long term. Those include narrowing WHO's focal priorities and finally resolving that WHO will interact in a more open, balanced and productive way with private industry, foundations, and nongovernmental groups. An inspector general and an overhaul of human-resource policies will bring WHO up to global standards.

How to carry forward this ambitious agenda? An interim WHO senior manager should be appointed in early 2016 to work through mid-2017. The selection of the next WHO director general (who will take office in June 2017 for a five-year term) will be pivotal. She or he needs to be a statesperson—someone with gravitas, dynamism, and skill in crisis management, mediation, organizational reform, strategic communications, and coalition building.

Several other very significant innovations are detailed in the Harvard Global Health Institute/London School of Hygiene and Tropical Medicine report. Reliable new financing mechanisms will build capacity, ensure quick response, and support long-term research and development. A UN Security Council Health Security Committee will strengthen high-level engagement. An Accountability Commission can provide independent expert oversight.

2016, Year of Decision

The year 2016 will be the test of whether it is at all feasible to execute reforms of the world's preparedness for dangerous infectious outbreaks. The deciding factor will not be knowing what needs to be done; the concrete reform agenda is known. It will be whether there is sustained, high-level political commitment.

34. Food Insecurity, Conflict, and Stability

Kimberly Flowers

Food insecurity is both a consequence and a cause of conflict, making it inexorably linked with political stability at regional, national, and international levels. Lack of access to affordable food has proven to trigger revolutions and spark unrest across the world. The first signs of the Arab Spring were riots in Algeria and Tunisia in 2011 over dramatic increases in the prices of dietary staples such as sugar, oil, and flour. The food-price crisis of 2007–2008 caused dozens of protests across the globe, serving as a wakeup call to the international community and the United States that investments in sustainable agricultural development are critical to political stability and national security.

Food should be considered a political commodity. It is often used as a strategic instrument of war, with evidence spanning from clashing groups in 1990s Sudan to Bashar al-Assad's war-torn Syria today. Agricultural markets sustain and stabilize many economies around the world, as well provide food to the hungry bellies of populations that may already be dissatisfied with high levels of unemployment, government corruption, or violence in their communities. Hungry populations are more likely to express frustration with troubled leadership, perpetuating a cycle of political instability and further undermining long-term economic development.

In 2016, regions within the Middle East and sub-Saharan Africa will be most sensitive to food insecurity, and several countries are likely to suffer political unrest and costly humanitarian crises because of their inability to meet their populations' basic food demands.

Syria is the biggest humanitarian crisis of this generation, and the situation continues to deteriorate. Nearly 10 million Syrians are unable to meet their daily food needs. The ongoing conflict has disrupted agricultural production, markets, and critical infrastructure, causing billions of dollars in damage that will take decades to reverse. Syria's GDP, once tied to a thriving agricultural sector, has been significantly compromised. A UN report in March of this year estimated total economic loss since the start of the conflict was more than $200 billion. Farmers are fleeing their lands indefinitely, and the massive refugee exodus is placing pressure on neighboring countries, from Jordan and Israel to many parts of Europe and the United States.

Evidence of food as a weapon of war is rampant across all factions and dimensions of the Syrian conflict. President Assad is waging a starvation campaign, purposely cutting populations off from humanitarian assistance. The Islamic State is using food as a recruitment tool, luring in weak citizens desperate for food and then folding vulnerable young men into their ranks. Points along the Turkey-Syria border that are used as aid-distribution sites have become violent hot spots controlled by armed men ready to use humanitarian aid as valuable leverage.

Meanwhile, Yemen is facing a possible famine brought on by the perfect storm of severe drought and violent conflict. Civil war threats from numerous rebel groups have exacerbated an already-weak system: before the crisis, 42 percent of the population was food insecure, the country imported over 90 percent of its food, and there was serious water scarcity. Now, a staggering 21 million people out of a population of 24.8 million are in need of urgent humanitarian assistance, including 13 million people who do not have enough to eat. In addition, the conflict escalated this year around the same time as the typical cropping season, from March to June, so the 2015 crop production will be much below average.

South Sudan's current crisis is a reminder of how important a reliable food system is to sustainable state building. Up to 95 percent of the population is dependent on agriculture for their livelihood, yet there is no underlying state infrastructure—roads and irrigation systems, for example—to support the agricultural industry. Today, an estimated 40 percent of the country cannot afford or access enough food to fulfill their daily needs, with populations facing emergency levels of acute food insecurity in conflict-affected areas. The dangerous combination of armed conflict, weak infrastructure, devalued currency, and soaring staple food prices could result in famine conditions in 2016 if South Sudan does not receive sufficient humanitarian aid.

Despite its impressive economic growth rates over the past decade, Nigeria has a delicate hold on food security in the northeastern part of the country due to the Islamic extremist group Boko Haram. Their brutal attacks, the government-led counterinsurgency, and ongoing ethnic clashes are responsible for displacing an estimated 1.5 to 2.5 million people, many of whom depend on agriculture for their livelihoods. Refugees who are able to return home often find their land, crops, and livestock destroyed. In a country where more than 60 percent of the massive and growing population lives in extreme poverty, these types of shocks have a deep impact.

Nigeria's import dependency does not help. It is the second-largest sugar, fish, and rice importer in the world, relying on large exporter countries like China to supply the 2 million metric tons of rice its population consumes each year. With food imports growing at an unsustainable rate of 11 percent and below-average staple crop yields three years in a row, Nigeria's food security is not stable enough to handle additional civil strife. Food insecurity will likely remain at emergency levels in northeast Nigeria well into 2016, pushing millions more in dire need of humanitarian aid.

Regional and international security will continue to impact and be fueled by the hunger levels of affected populations. Building food security in countries like Syria, Yemen, South Sudan, and Nigeria is complex and costly. The United States has defined itself as a leader in addressing global food security. Now is the time to sustain that commitment to countries that need it the most.

35. Normalization and Human Rights in Cuba

Carl Meacham

In December 2015, Presidents Barack Obama and Raul Castro announced a historic change: the United States and Cuba would begin to normalize their bilateral relationship, opening formal diplomatic channels between the two countries for the first time in decades.

So much has happened in the intervening months. The two presidents met in person at the Summit of the Americas. The White House unilaterally eased travel to Cuba and removed the island from the U.S. list of state sponsors of terrorism. The U.S. embassy in Havana and the Cuban embassy in Washington reopened, and Cuban ambassador Cabañas recently became an officially credentialed representative of the Cuban government in the United States.

The progress is exciting—but it's important to remember that the two countries are just getting started. There's a long road to travel before the bilateral relationship is truly normalized, and many thorny issues remain to be addressed. Two in particular stand out: the decades-old Cuban expropriations of U.S. property holdings on the island; and the Castro brothers' poor human-rights record.

It's the human-rights situation that garners the most criticism here in the United States. Political dissidents are regularly imprisoned, the country has lacked even a semblance of democracy for decades, and Cubans are systematically denied civil rights.

Pope Francis's recent visit to Cuba is a reminder of that tough human-rights reality on the island. Cuban dissidents were denied attendance at papal events, which the pope acknowledged, referencing "all those who, for various reasons, [he would] not be able to meet."

His acknowledgment of the ongoing human-rights troubles in Cuba is key, particularly given his role in mediating the bilateral talks that led to the normalization announcement last December. Mentioning the dissidents was, however subtle, a nod to what has long been a priority of U.S. policy toward Cuba: seeing repression decrease and human rights actively protected by the Cuban government.

For decades, the U.S. government has pointed to human-rights concerns as a primary driver of U.S. policy toward Cuba. Decades of pushing for democratic change through isolation ultimately proved fruitless, with Cubans no freer in 2014 than in the 1960s. And this is where the developing normalization process may make a real difference.

In the lead-up to the pope's visit, the Cuban government announced the release of over 3,500 prisoners in a gesture of good faith (although, to be fair, many worry that the gesture was an empty one). We can't know yet if it was a real step forward, but we do know that it was one of the largest releases of prisoners since Fidel Castro took power in 1959.

The changing bilateral relationship has the potential to create real change. For the normalization process to be credible, the two countries must work together to address human rights. And it seems increasingly likely that they'll do just that.

The first reason is simple: for the first time in decades, they can. With bilateral dialogues underway since December of last year, channels of communication are finally open. And there's nothing excluding human-rights concerns from those channels.

The second is more nuanced: human rights are no less a priority of U.S. foreign policy in Cuba than they were before, but now, Washington can speak from an informed vantage point on the reality on the ground in Cuba—and on what needs to change. What's more, we can rally the region behind us—a region that long opposed U.S. isolation of Cuba, despite also looking unfavorably on the practices of the Castros' government. After decades of the opposite, the region will no longer regard the United States as part of the problem. Regional support will only make U.S. efforts to highlight Cuba's challenges more powerful. Nothing roots out injustice as efficiently as shining a light on it, and we finally have access to the switch.

No one knows this better than the Cuban government—an institution with more factions than ever willing to begin to consider change primarily out of economic necessity, but with a massive infrastructure designed to prevent just that. That same infrastructure made the Cuban government difficult to bring to the table and on board with the normalization process.

That isn't to say that Washington is united on the issue, either. Many of the very people that would be best equipped to bridge the gap between the two countries—prominent Cuban Americans, and elected officials in particular—are the quickest to criticize the new relationship rather than realizing the tremendous potential to advance the cause of human rights granted by the new policy.

For all that the old policy toward Cuba undoubtedly had the right priorities, it was a policy that tied our hands behind our back. A very long cold shoulder brought about little in the way of change that advanced U.S. priorities on the island. Normalization will not be without setbacks. But, we're seeing some signs that more will be obtained with dialogue than through isolation.

36. Winning the War of Ideas

Farah Pandith and Juan Zarate

There is a broad consensus that the United States and the West are losing the messaging war against the Islamic State, al-Qaeda, and like-minded terrorists. Indeed, there has been much focus on terrorists' use of social media to spread their message and attract thousands of followers from the heart of the Middle East to America's heartland.

The challenge from this ideology and global movement, however, is often reduced to a problem of messaging or public diplomacy. The reality is that we are losing more than just a battle in the media and on the Internet.

We are losing the broader "battle of ideas" against a violent extremist ideology that is infecting a whole new generation of Muslim millennials and defining what it means to be Muslim in the twenty-first century. In failing to recognize this broader challenge, we are failing to confront the real-world manifestations of this ideology.

The Islamic State—with its wanton barbarity and declared "caliphate"—represents the latest manifestation of an ideological movement birthed by al-Qaeda. The underlying terrorist manifesto and heroic mythology of a religious obligation to fight against an assault on Muslims is heralded through ideological outposts in satellite sermons, garage mosque meetings, and Facebook friends. With a vast recruitment pipeline, slick media products, and targeted use of social media, new recruits and identities are forming.

With 62 percent of 1.6 billion Muslims worldwide under the age of 30, this is a generational threat. And the terrorists know this—using schools, videos, and terror—to inculcate a new generation with their message. Some children attending ISIS-controlled schools have been reported to declare, "ISIS is like Disneyland."

In concert, ISIS is recruiting young girls and women to drive the spread of the ideology in new families while dispatching women to ISIS outposts well beyond Syria and Iraq to help regenerate radicalization. The radicalization of women and their willingness to become involved in all phases of terrorist operations is worrying security officials and families around the world.

But it's the survival of the "Islamic caliphate" and continued ISIS governance in major Middle Eastern cities and territory that fuels the underlying romantic vision of this identity and a medieval Islamic state. It's the ability of extremists to intimidate and force ideological change that is impacting globally.

This violent ideological movement is altering the political landscape and erasing national borders. In so doing, they are destroying evidence of peoples, history, and culture that threaten their worldview. If they succeed, the world will lose proof of the diversity of religious belief, including within Islam, and the heritage of ancient civilizations.

The destruction of peoples and heritage represents these extremists' ideological battle brought to life. This requires societies to embrace and defend historical diversity like antibodies as a bulwark against modern extremist division.

We must save persecuted minorities and the threatened sacred sites—from revered tombs and ancient monasteries in the Middle East to temples and statues in Asia. This involves helping mobilize a set of actors and networks already committed to the preservation of peoples, texts, and languages—including archaeologists, heritage trusts, museums, and libraries.

Extremism also threatens to silence courageous moderate voices. Terrorists have assassinated writers and activists in Muslim societies challenging violent extremist orthodoxy. In Bangladesh this past year, moderate bloggers have been butchered in front of loved ones. These voices have to be amplified, networked, and protected.

The baseline ideology is slowly erasing the richness of local cultures—replacing the colorful, traditional clothes and lifestyles of women from Africa to Central and Southeast Asia. And their attacks are deepening social and political fissures, even changing the shape of Western societies—with attacks like those in Paris that accelerate Jewish migration from France.

The embedding of this ideology in conflict zones can track with the outbreak of disease. These extremists have often helped polio re-emerge in hotspots—like northern Nigeria, western Pakistan, Syria, and Somalia—where their ideology teaches that vaccines are a plot by the West to harm Muslims. Vaccination teams have been banned, harassed, and even killed. The international health community and those like the Rotary Foundation committed to the eradication of polio need to be supported, with Muslim clerics, leaders, and countries finding ways to deliver vaccinations and counter the false narrative of the extremists.

This ideology has also spawned some of the worst human-rights abuses and war crimes in the twenty-first century—from mass executions and attempted genocide to the institutionalization of sexual slavery and child soldiers. Merely documenting the atrocities or having #BringBackOurGirls go viral to raise awareness of Boko Haram abductees should not comfort us. The human-rights community needs to find more effective, sustainable, and creative ways to deter and counter the spread of such atrocities and their animating ideology.

Terrorist groups are putting the environment at risk as well. There is growing concern that militant groups of all stripes—to include al-Shabaab, the al-Qaeda affiliate in Somalia—are funding their conflicts through the industrialized poaching trade in Africa, fueled by exploding demand in China and Asia. Elephants, rhinos, and other endangered species are at imminent risk. This requires a concerted global effort—to curb demand, dismantle networks, interdict shipments, and protect the animals and their ecosystems. The administration's strategy to confront wildlife trafficking aggressively is an important but insufficient step.

Through two administrations, the United States has struggled to counter this ideology. The U.S. government is neither expert nor credible in confronting an ideology grounded in interpretations of Islam. Yet we cannot abdicate taking the ideological fight to the enemy nor hope that these groups will alienate themselves into extinction with their brutality.

Muslims themselves—to include our allies in Muslim-majority nations, local leaders, and communities—must confront this problem directly, deny it funding, while also defining and respecting modern, diverse Muslim identities. This requires curtailing and challenging the most extreme dimensions of radical Islamic proselytizing and recruitment globally.

But we cannot simply assume that our allies—especially in Muslim communities—can defend against the threat of terror and the allure of the ideology on their own. America must lead—empowering, enabling, and defending networks, communities, and individuals willing to confront the ideology.

The White House and United Nations summits to counter violent extremism held in 2015 were opportunities to advance a serious, dedicated campaign to undermine the credibility of the terrorist ideology. Though important, the summits did not recognize fully that the world must confront directly the outbreaks and manifestations of this ideology—like it does a pandemic.

This requires empowering a new type of coalition—a network of networks—that not only counters the extremists' narrative and seeks to intervene and replace it, but also gets ahead of it through inoculation. How? We must first directly confront the sources and manifestations of the radical ideology plaguing the world.

Former extremists have organized to counter recruitment and the ideology on the streets, in campuses, and online. Attempts to amplify these and other credible voices and create new platforms for expression and a sense of modern identity not dictated by terrorists—like local radio programs run by kids in Mali or street theater in Luton, UK—have worked on a small scale. All of these efforts must be scaled up dramatically.

And the new and virulent manifestations of these threats offer opportunities to create new alliances and networks to confront the ideology—from human-rights and women's groups to archaeologists and conservationists. International security forces and private stability operations teams could be enlisted to protect vulnerable populations, sites, individuals, and species against violent extremists.

This ideological fight is not just about terrorism. These are enemies of humanity—attempting to spread their ideology like a virus while reshaping borders, history, and identity. It's time for a new coalition of global actors to take on and win this generational fight. This will require more than just creative messaging. It demands stopping the manifestations of the ideology itself.

Contributors

JON B. ALTERMAN is senior vice president, holds the Zbigniew Brzezinski Chair in Global Security and Geostrategy, and is director of the Middle East Program at CSIS.

ERNEST Z. BOWER is a senior adviser, Sumitro Chair for Southeast Asia Studies, and codirector of the Pacific Partners Initiative at CSIS.

MARK CANCIAN is a senior adviser with the International Security Program at CSIS.

VICTOR CHA is a senior adviser and Korea Chair at CSIS and a professor of government and director of Asian studies at Georgetown University.

EDWARD C. CHOW is a senior fellow in the Energy and National Security Program at CSIS.

CRAIG COHEN is executive vice president at CSIS.

LISA COLLINS is a fellow with the Korea Chair at CSIS.

HEATHER A. CONLEY is senior vice president for Europe, Eurasia, and the Arctic and director of the Europe Program at CSIS.

JENNIFER G. COOKE is director of the Africa Program at CSIS.

ANTHONY H. CORDESMAN holds the Arleigh A. Burke Chair in Strategy at CSIS.

MELISSA G. DALTON is a fellow and the chief of staff in the International Security Program at CSIS.

KIMBERLY FLOWERS is director of the Global Food Security Project at CSIS.

MATTHEW FUNAIOLE is a fellow with the China Power Project at CSIS.

BONNIE S. GLASER is a senior adviser for Asia and the director of the China Power Project at CSIS.

MATTHEW P. GOODMAN holds the William E. Simon Chair in Political Economy at CSIS.

MICHAEL J. GREEN is senior vice president for Asia and holds the Japan Chair at CSIS and is an associate professor at the Walsh School of Foreign Service at Georgetown University.

SHANNON N. GREEN is a senior fellow and director of the Human Rights Initiative at CSIS.

JOHN J. HAMRE is president and CEO, Pritzker Chair, and director of the Brzezinski Institute at CSIS.

TODD HARRISON is the director of defense budget analysis and a senior fellow in the International Security Program at CSIS.

REBECCA K.C. HERSMAN is director of the Project on Nuclear Issues and senior adviser in the CSIS International Security Program.

KATHLEEN H. HICKS is a senior vice president, holds the Henry A. Kissinger chair, and directs the International Security Program at CSIS.

ANDREW HUNTER is a senior fellow in the International Security Program and director of the Defense-Industrial Initiatives Group at CSIS.

CHRISTOPHER K. JOHNSON is a senior adviser and holds the Freeman Chair in China Studies at CSIS.

THOMAS KARAKO is a senior fellow with the International Security Program and the director of the Missile Defense Project at CSIS.

SCOTT KENNEDY is deputy director of the Freeman Chair in China Studies and director of the Project on Chinese Business and Political Economy at CSIS.

SARAH O. LADISLAW is a senior fellow and director of the Energy and National Security Program at CSIS.

JAMES A. LEWIS is a senior fellow and director of the Strategic Technologies Program at CSIS.

HAIM MALKA is a senior fellow and deputy director of the Middle East Program at CSIS.

JEFFREY MANKOFF is a senior fellow and deputy director of the Russia and Eurasia Program at CSIS.

CARL MEACHAM is the director of the Americas Program at CSIS.

SCOTT MILLER is senior adviser and holds the William M. Scholl Chair in International Business at CSIS.

J. STEPHEN MORRISON is a senior vice president and director of the Global Health Policy Center at CSIS.

SEAN O'KEEFE is a distinguished senior adviser at CSIS and the Phanstiel Chair in Strategic Management and Leadership at the Maxwell School of Syracuse University.

OLGA OLIKER is a senior adviser and director of the Russia and Eurasia Program at CSIS.

FARAH PANDITH is a senior fellow at Harvard University's Kennedy School of Government and was the State Department's first ever special representative to Muslim communities.

JEFFREY RATHKE is a senior fellow and deputy director of the Europe Program at CSIS.

RICHARD M. ROSSOW is a senior fellow and holds the Wadhwani Chair in U.S.-India Policy Studies at CSIS.

DANIEL F. RUNDE is director of the Project on Prosperity and Development and holds the William A. Schreyer Chair in Global Analysis at CSIS.

THOMAS SANDERSON is a senior fellow and director of the Transnational Threats Project at CSIS.

SHARON SQUASSONI is a senior fellow and director of the Proliferation Prevention Program at CSIS.

FRANK A. VERRASTRO is a senior vice president and holds the James R. Schlesinger Chair for Energy & Geopolitics at CSIS.

JUAN ZARATE is a senior adviser with the Transnational Threats Project and the Homeland Security and Counterterrorism Program at CSIS.

DENISE E. ZHENG is a senior fellow and deputy director of the Strategic Technologies Program at CSIS.

Index

 <!-- Generator: Adobe Illustrator 19.1.0, SVG Export Plug-In -->
<svg version="1.1" xmlns="http://www.w3.org/2000/svg" xmlns:xlink="http://www.w3.org/1999/xlink" xmlns:a="http://ns.adobe.com/AdobeSVGViewerExtensions/3.0/" x="0px" y="0px" width="87px" height="87px" viewBox="0 0 87 87" style="overflow:scroll;enable-background:new 0 0 87 87;" xml:space="preserve">
<style type="text/css">
  .st0{fill:none;stroke:#005068;stroke-width:12;stroke-linecap:round;stroke-dasharray:0;}
</style>
<defs>
</defs>
<rect x="18.7" y="18.7" transform="matrix(0.7071 0.7071 -0.7071 0.7071 43.4871 -18.0129)" class="st0" width="49.5" height="49.5"/>
</svg>

86–87
wartime combat operations,
86
and mobilization against Ebola,
133–134
nuclear program of, 99
nuclear weapons reductions, 103
oil production, 110–111
paradoxical status as superpower
with lessening global influence,
7–8, 13–14
position in Asia-Pacific, 61, 62
power grid in, cyber reconnaissance and, 106–107
space programs, Russia and,
95–96
trade with China, Chinese economic slowdown and, 56
UN Security Council, and response to
infectious outbreaks, 136–137
U.S. Agency for International Development, and Ebola epidemic,
133–134
USAID. *See* U.S. Agency for International Development

V

Vaccination, extremists' opposition
to, 146
Venezuela
energy sector in, 111–112
repressive practices and, 124
Vietnam
geopolitical importance of, 61
Russian arms sales to, 48
Vietnam War, damage to American
influence from, 13
Violent extremism
countermeasures against, 147–148
and war of ideas, 144–148

W

Walker, Darren, 127

War, versus engagement, 11
War crimes, extremists', 146
War funding, U.S., 84–86
West Africa, Ebola in, mobilization
against, 133–134
West Bengal, elections, 2016, 65–68
Westphalian system, 2
Women, radicalization of, by ISIS, 145
World Bank
AIIB as rival to, 59
and climate change, 14, 117
World Health Organization (WHO)
Center for Emergency Prepared-
ness and Response, 136
director general of, 137
and Ebola epidemic, 133
emergency capacities, strengthen-
ing of, 136–137
reform of, 136–137

X

Xi Jinping, 47
anticorruption drive, 52–53
as fair-weather reformer, 51, 56
foreign policy of, 58
mid-term challenges faced by,
50–53
reform vision of, 50–52, 55, 56–57
vision of "Asia for Asians," 58

Y

Yanukovych, Viktor, 38, 39–40, 48
Yemen
energy sector in, 111
food insecurity in, 139
Iran's influence in, 28
U.S. vision and strategy for, 27
Yeonpyeong island, 70
Yuan, Sino-Russian trade and, 46

Z

Zimbabwe, repressive practices and,
124

About CSIS

For over 50 years, the Center for Strategic and International Studies (CSIS) has worked to develop solutions to the world's greatest policy challenges. Today, CSIS scholars are providing strategic insights and bipartisan policy solutions to help decisionmakers chart a course toward a better world.

CSIS is a nonprofit organization headquartered in Washington, D.C. The Center's 220 full-time staff and large network of affiliated scholars conduct research and analysis and develop policy initiatives that look into the future and anticipate change.

Founded at the height of the Cold War by David M. Abshire and Admiral Arleigh Burke, CSIS was dedicated to finding ways to sustain American prominence and prosperity as a force for good in the world. Since 1962, CSIS has become one of the world's preeminent international institutions focused on defense and security; regional stability; and transnational challenges ranging from energy and climate to global health and economic integration.

Thomas J. Pritzker was named chairman of the CSIS Board of Trustees in November 2015. Former U.S. deputy secretary of defense John J. Hamre has served as the Center's president and chief executive officer since 2000.

CSIS does not take specific policy positions; accordingly, all views expressed herein should be understood to be solely those of the author(s).